The Power of Giving

Through Giving Create Wealth and Abundance

Ersin Sirer

Published by Dolman Scott in 2022

Copyright2020©Ersin Sirer

Cover Design by Mehmet Akduman www.akdumancreative.co.uk

The authors assert the moral right under the Copyright, Designs and Patents Act 1988 to be identified as the authors of this work. All rights reserved. No part of this publication may be reproduced, stored in a retrieval system, or transmitted, in any form or by any means without the prior written consent of the authors, nor be otherwise circulated in any form of binding or cover, other than that in which it is published and without a similar condition being imposed on the subsequent purchaser.

978-1-915351-02-9 – PoD

978-1-915351-03-6 – eBook

Published by
Dolman Scott
www.dolmanscott.com

"Do your little bit of good where you are; it's those little bits of good put together that overwhelm the world"

– Desmond Tutu

Dedication

I dedicate this book to the silent global force of volunteer charity workers who devote their lives for the betterment of their fellow human. With nearly two billion people living in extreme poverty earning just over a dollar a day, and over 600 million people going to bed on an empty stomach each night, we must all reach out with love and giving to all in need.

Foreword

Hestia is a charity working each year with over 10,000 adults and children in crisis, across London and the South-East. Since March 2020, under lockdown and the restrictions of the COVID-19 pandemic, many of us have rediscovered in unexpected ways the things in our lives that really matter. Many have rediscovered that relationships and generosity trump possessions and selfishness. The joy of 'giving back' or even 'giving away' have emerged as, often ignored, core human needs which are deeply satisfying.

Ersin's new book reminds us that all organisations have a strong vested interest in fostering a giving culture. A willingness to help others achieve their goals lies at the heart of effective collaboration, innovation, quality improvement and service excellence. He draws to our attention that successful givers produced 50% more annual revenue, on average, than colleagues who focused less on helping others, and that new research has revealed that the more SMEs give to charity, the stronger their business performs. Overall, 68 percent of businesses that give to charity reported a positive impact on profitability. Ersin's book covers social, personal and business giving and incentivises the reader to making giving a part of their lives.

This joy and deep satisfaction which is to be found in generosity and giving are not, however, a recent discovery for Ersin. His support for those in his friendship circles as well as those far beyond is known to all. At Hestia, his regular

meetings and workshops with men and women who are at a low point in their lives are filled with sensitivity, respect, optimism, warmth and hope. His new book reminds us all that we are relational creatures; what happens to others – at some level happens to all of us, and that generosity and giving are deeply rewarding activities that give us the experience of community and belonging which we all crave and need.
    Patrick Ryan
    CEO
    Hestia
    www.hestia.org

"No person was ever honoured for what he received. Honour has been the reward for what he gave"

– **President Calvin Coolidge**

Contents

Dedication iv

Foreword v

Introduction 1

My Back Story 2
   About The Author 2
   Business 3
   Mentoring & Charity 4
   Author 5
   Why Am I Writing this Book? 6

What is Giving? 7
   First Give to Yourself 8
   Setting Personal Goals 9
   Giving to Yourself versus Selfishness 9
   Give to Yourself Self-Belief 11
   Seeing Everything as It Is 12
   How Can We Give? 14
   The Power of Commitment 15
   Come Out of Your Comfort Zone 17
   Fear is Limiting – Stops Us Giving 18
   The Uncertainty of Life is the Only Certainty 19
   Acceptance 19
   Do Not Try to Control 21

Give Hope and Love 22
    What is Hope? 23
    Hope is Essential 23
    People Have the Potential to Do Great Things –
        inspire them! 24
    No Hope – Leads to Suicide, the Ultimate
        Escape 25
    How to Give Hope 25
    How do You Keep Hope? 26
    Give Unconditional Love 26

Why Should We Give? 29
    The Giver 29
    Giving to Your Family 30
    Teaching Your Children Giving 30
    Giving and Understanding Kids 32
    How to Help Kids Learn to Love Giving 32

What Are the Benefits of Giving? 35
    Why Giving Makes You Happy 36
    What to Give 39

What is the Power of Giving? 40
    Altruism: The Miracle Drug 40
    Giving Has Immense Personal Benefits 43
    Quotes About the Power of Giving 44
    Cycle of Giving 46

The Power of Generosity 46
Community Giving 49

Take Responsibility and Own Your Actions 51
What Does it Mean to Take Responsibility for
　Your Actions? 51
Happiness is a Choice 53
We Can't Ignore Our Emotions 53
Quotes from Celebrated People About
　Responsibility 56
Asking Can Be Giving 59

**How Does Giving Work Within the Business and
Professional World?** 60
Most Successful Leaders Are Givers 63
Looking Out for the Greatest Good 64

Communication is a Powerful Tool in Giving 66
Public Speaking and Giving 68
Public Speeches That Had a Profound Effect
　in History 68

Givers and Takers 72
Takers 72
Givers 72
Matchers 73
Who Are Achieving the Most? 73
How Do You Spot a Taker? 75

Giving and Collaboration 77
What Can Givers Do to Avoid Burn-out? 77
Smartness in the Way You Give 78
How to Be a Successful Giver 79
Receiving Is Harder Than Giving 80
Some Reasons Why Receiving Is Often More
    Difficult Than Giving 80
Practice Non-Judgement 82
Laziness and How to Eliminate It 83
Give All At Once 85
How Should You Give? 85

Caring 86
Caring in a Business Environment 87
Sharing is Giving 87
Individualism versus Collectivism 89

Giving Creates Abundance 90
Create Unlimited Opportunities 91

Give Meditation Time to Yourself 95
Mindfulness 97
Help Someone 98

Gratitude 99
Gratefulness is Uplifting 100

Philanthropy 103
   What Qualifies Someone to be a
      Philanthropist?.. 103
   What is the Role of Philanthropy? 103
   Who Started Philanthropy?.. 104
   Corporate Philanthropy.. 104
   The 13 Most Philanthropic Companies in the
      World... 104
   Who Are Some Famous Philanthropists?................ 106
   Quotes from Famous Philanthropists...................... 109
   Further Quotes of Wisdom....................................... 110
   Famous Charity Workers 114

Global Growth & Giving 120
   WORLD'S TOP 10 MOST GENEROUS
      COUNTRIES... 120
   Methodology 122
   The World's Most Generous Countries 123
   Other Top Generous Countries 124
   Obsession with Economic Growth.......................... 125
   Questioning the Growth Model............................... 128
   Vision for Leadership in Business 130
   Principles of Ethical Work Practices....................... 130
   Social Capitalism.. 132

What Does Social Capitalism Look Like? 133

Circular Economy to Save the World.......................... 137

Benefits of Organisational Giving ... 141
Giving Something Back: raising the profile of your business through good works ... 142
The Business Benefits of Giving ... 143
Giving to Your Employees ... 144

Make Giving a Part of Your Life ... 146
Find Your Passion ... 147
Give Your Time ... 147
Find Ways to Integrate Your Interests and Skills with the Needs of Others ... 147
Be Proactive, Not Reactive ... 148
Purpose, Meaning and Happiness ... 148

Thank You ... 149
Supported Charitable Organisations ... 150

References ... 152

Also by Ersin Sirer

Property Development & HMO Investment Success

Treating Tenants as clients and working with a conscience

Introduction

I have been fortunate to experience some wonderful sharing moments, most were unplanned and spontaneous, within the context of these moments so has the idea of writing a book evolved. I hope you will enjoy "The Power of Giving" as much as I have enjoyed writing it.

My Back Story

About The Author

The book is not about me, but I think it's important for the reader to have an idea about the author.

I was born in Istanbul in 1963 with little schooling in Turkey, and not speaking a word of English arrived in London in the winter of 1969, this was to be the start of my life in the UK.

My father, mother and I were immigrants in a foreign country with a different culture, language, and weather, I remember it rained every day for two weeks when we arrived.

My late father was a hard-working person from a village in north eastern Turkey. He started working at the age of 12 as a bell-boy in a hotel to help support his family, and prior to coming to London at the age of 33 had risen to the position of assistant General Manager of a well-known five-star Istanbul hotel.

My father's ambitions led him within a few years of his arrival in the UK, to set up in the mid 70's one of the first Turkish restaurant chains in London, and with the exception of a major heart attack at the age of 42, he worked non-stop for 69 years until his death aged 80, a self-made and self-educated businessman and most importantly a kind giving person.

I have few positive memories from my childhood, I was an immigrant with few friends, so I had deep periods of loneliness, always in the corner on my own, it seemed. I resolved never to treat anyone as insignificant, and never knowingly have. My secondary school was tough, gangs were prevalent, but I pushed myself to be the best the that I could be, I consistently received high marks and excellent reports, and became a model student. I was personally commended by the headmaster several times. Then I came crashing back down to earth. At the age of 14, I was present at a parents' evening when my bubble was burst. One teacher told my parents, "It doesn't matter how hard Ersin works, he will never become good at this subject." Those words shattered me, and completely demotivated me. Hence, as an adult I have never put anyone down; my daily ambition is to lift people and make them feel good about themselves.

Business

I have been a businessman for nearly 40 years. Initially in the restaurant sector, owning and operating a chain of restaurants in central London. One of the restaurants that I operated for 35 years was in Chelsea, it was called Chelsea Bun, it was frequented by many well-known celebrities like Bob Geldof, Kylie Minogue, Minnie Driver, Martina Navratilova and many others, it became a restaurant institution in West London, until it's closure in May 2019.

In 1994 I branched out into the property sector, investing and developing properties, completing close to 100 projects. These range from high-end luxury properties, selling for over £5 million, to lower priced stock with unit sales prices of £200,000. Projects included conversions from office or warehouse to residential, new build and reconstruction of old properties. My philosophy is to source good plots, contract credible construction firms, and bring together a professional team. I am also an investor in long-term residential property, focused mainly on Houses of Multiple Occupancy. The HMO business model emphasis is to purchase properties at below market value, developing these to increase the internal area, creating more lettable room space, thus increasing the gross revenue.

I am also a business development consultant, using my wide network of contacts and business experience to assist people and companies expand their investments and businesses both in the UK and internationally.

Mentoring and Charity

I am involved with several charities, the main one is Hestia. It is one of the largest providers of domestic-abuse refuges in London and the South-East, and the main organisation supporting victims of modern slavery in the capital. My involvement is in raising awareness to this charity, assisting with fundraising, and visits to the refuges to give motivational workshops.

I also work internationally through mentoring and raising awareness in the Dar Lekbira Orphanage in Morocco. This orphanage has been established for several years in Kenitra, a city which is located close to the capital, Rabat. It houses and supports over 120 orphaned children, teenagers and young adults.

"We can create a great society by creating great people, not the other way around."

Author

My published book is **Property Development and HMO Investment Success,** *Treating Tenants as clients and working with a conscience.* This is a guide book on property developing and House of Multiple Occupation investments; however, most importantly it is a guide on doing business in an ethical way, treating tenants as clients, building positive and credible relationships; homelessness and how to eradicate it, and much more.

Why Am I Writing this Book?

Over the years the subject-matter of giving has evolved within my daily life. Initially, it was unconscious, but in the past few years it has become a conscious giving to the point where I make a concerted effort daily to give, and to give as many times as I feel I can.

The giving must be genuine and for real situations, not just for the sake of giving. The giving must do good, in whatever way it can benefit the other person.

What does giving mean and how does it affect the person one gives to, how does it affect the giver, why we should give, why is giving not so prevalent in our world, and why is there expectation attached to giving.?

Within this thinking process so have the seeds of writing a book evolved. What does this book mean to me and why am I writing it? It firstly allows me to structure and compile all my thoughts and experiences; secondly and most importantly, it allows me to share these with others: it's a platform from which others can pick up ideas, learn and make it their own, to ultimately use and benefit their lives. Once giving becomes a part of a person's life, the student will become the giver and teach others the wonders of giving and the many benefits it gives back to the giver.

What is Giving?

The word giving has a primary association for most people linked to charity, and the giving of money. As important and valuable as this form of giving is, it is only one of the many ways of giving we can participate in; without the process of giving and taking humankind would not exist.

I would describe the process of giving by first making sure we understand why we are giving, and the reason we are giving must be relevant to the person or organisation we are giving to. The question must be asked: who is that person, what do we know about them? Hence, before the act of giving there must be empathy and the desire to get to know the recipient. Every person has a different need, and this extends to professional and business life, too; therefore, by first listening, observing and learning, we are able to understand their needs and thereby decide on why to give and how to give.

Giving can be described as the act of thoughtful actions towards a person which will bring positive and constructive benefit to their life. The benefits can be one of many things: financial gain, feeling of well-being, happiness, health, friendship, security, improving self-worth, and many others. The continual act of giving can "ONLY" bring enhancement to the quality of life of the recipient and enrich the inner well-being of the person who is giving, "The Giver".

First Give to Yourself

The most important relationship you will ever have is the relationship you have with yourself. In order to genuinely love others, we need to love ourselves first. We need to cultivate self-acceptance and strengthen our self-esteem.

We need to be receiving from ourselves. This does not have to be for any special reason or event, but just because you are worthwhile and important. You deserve to treat yourself as well as you treat others. You deserve to be a priority: you're valuable as a person.

We often do not associate giving to ourselves; however, we must start here, because it is vital to give to yourself. I am not talking about being selfish or self-obsessed – giving to yourself is a positive and constructive act. Selfishness implies a disregard for others. Self-giving, on the other hand, implies a positive regard for yourself.

For example, if your best friend calls you to say they are feeling really dizzy and sick, and needs to go to the doctor, but you were about to start a Netflix show you'd been looking forward to watching! Disregarding your friend when they are having a crisis, just to fulfil your own desires, would be very selfish.

On the other hand, taking time out of your day (this is your life, after all) to spend time cherishing yourself is self-giving. If you get home from work and you want to watch that TV show, take a walk, write a journal about your day, or take a bath; it's a worthwhile use of your time. You are giving a gift from yourself to yourself. The focus is on uplifting your life in a personal way.

Setting Personal Goals

First map out your future goals, decide on your objectives; this will put structure and a foundation to your life. This can be explained simply, like saying when you start your car journey to go from A to B, how will you get to B when you have not even decided where B is going to be? Once you decide where B will be as your destination, you will then be able to map out your route. En route you will see the countryside, wildlife, new towns, meet people and help them in any way that you can; however, you are still moving to your chosen destination whilst interacting with all there is around you in your journey. One can use this analogy for one's life, too: we must have life goals and realistic objectives, set up short-term incremental steps to reach our long-term objectives. Life is about living in a fulfilling, purposeful way, creating consciousness of everything around us and giving in an instinctive way.

Giving to Yourself versus Selfishness

I would describe the difference between selfishness and giving to yourself as follows:

When someone behaves in a manner that's self-serving, there is an underlying singularly selfish intent that simply isn't present with self-care. Being selfish means there's a desire to take from others to their detriment, whereas self-care is about replenishing your resources without depleting someone else's. Someone who is selfish cares only about themselves and doesn't consider others. If your actions are selfish, they all have to do with getting something for yourself only.

As people, we only have a finite amount of resources with which to operate, so taking care of ourselves really isn't a matter of selfishness; in fact, making sure our own needs are met only makes us more well-equipped to support others. There are stark differences between taking care of yourself and taking from others to make yourself feel better.

When you take time to rest and do things that help restore your energy, you're much healthier on all fronts, which could have a positive impact on everything in your life, from relationships to job performance and negative habits.

Self-care involves setting boundaries so you don't expend all of your personal energy taking care of everyone but yourself.

Once you get the hang of showing yourself love without apologising for it, you'll notice an increase in security that comes with knowing you can provide for yourself. In contrast, selfishness is rooted in an unspoken insecurity that wrongly convinces you that you'll never have enough.

Selfishness excludes others, whereas self-care does not.

It's not uncommon for people to feel left out or abandoned when you don't accommodate them, but realise it's in *your* best interest to not stretch yourself too thinly. Self-care is just as critical a sustenance as drinking water and eating food, and our survival depends on it.

Give to Yourself Self-Belief

Confidence and self-belief are vital in approaching any challenge; if you do not believe in yourself, how would you expect anyone else to? With self-belief there also must be focus, action and the ability to make others believe in your dreams.

People cannot achieve their goals without self-belief, and along the way convince others to join in their journey.

Self-confidence means to have faith or trust in yourself.

Nobody is born with limitless self-confidence. If someone seems to have incredible self-confidence, it's because he or she has worked on building it for years. Self-confidence is something that you learn to build up, because the challenging world of business, and life in general, can deflate it. Well-meaning but sometimes unkind comments from those closest to us can also hit us hard.

On top of this, we have to deal with our inner critic of self-doubt that constantly tells us that we are not good enough. When bombarded by so many elements that threaten our self-confidence, we need to take charge of building it up for ourselves.

Visualise yourself as you want to be
"What the mind can conceive and believe it can achieve"

– Napoleon Hill

Affirm yourself
"Affirmations are a powerful tool to deliberately install desired beliefs about yourself"

– Nikki Carnevale

Question your inner critic
"You have been criticising yourself for years, and it hasn't worked. Try approving of yourself and see what happens"

– Louise L. Hay

Set yourself up to win
"To establish true self-confidence, we must concentrate on our successes and forget about the failures and the negatives in our lives"

– Denis Waitley

Seeing Everything As It Is

Most of us don't notice impermanence until it's shoved in our face. We're too busy, too focused on having and doing.

Death is, of course, the paradigm of all change. People are dying all around us, but we don't see it happening; we don't want to see it, and for the most part we manage to keep it hidden. Back in the 1970s, the writer Ernest Becker won a Pulitzer Prize for his book *The Denial of Death*, in which he argued that American society is fundamentally committed to not seeing death. Yet, in India, where dying and death are everywhere in full view, there is a sense of relief that comes from the direct encounter with a universal truth, no matter how unpleasant that truth might be.

To see things as they really are means to see them consistently in an unbiased, non-judgemental light. Not to see them in this way, or to deceive oneself about their reality and range of application, is the defining mark of ignorance, and ignorance is by itself a potent cause of suffering, knitting the net in which man is caught – the net of false hopes, of unrealistic and harmful desires, of delusive ideologies and of perverted values and aims.

We go through life from childhood being bombarded by others' views, guidance and personal agendas; the media and society, too, are complicit in trying to educate and influence, to make us think in a certain way. However, the important fact is that we must, as much as humanly possible, look upon people and situations without bias and without pre-conceived ideas, not to judge; we must accept differences of opinion. This allows us to make better decisions based on the here and now and seeing everything as it really is, without allowing religion, our friends, or family to influence us.

Those whose minds are filled with fear, anxieties, desires and expectations, find it hard to understand. They cannot see the truth because they are not ready for it. They do not understand it because they have become comfortable with the illusions that have become integral to their personalities. Most of us take things for granted. We go through the motions of life as if we know everything about it already and as if we have gone through it already. We hardly see. We hardly pay attention. We rarely stay with the moment. We are stuck somewhere either in the past or in the future, with some notion, fear, fantasy, idea or illusion. We do not see things as they are, but according to our mental states. Our judging, calculating and measuring minds get in the way of our seeing and knowing.

Our thinking stands in between ourselves and the reality around us. Our perceptions, conclusions, knowledge and the so-called wisdom we acquire through analysis and conditioning, may give us the satisfaction that we have achieved some erudition or intellectual superiority, but in truth we remain as ignorant as ever because we have not learned to open ourselves to the beauty and the truth that surrounds us.

How Can We Give?

"Give what you can afford to give in time, guidance, assistance and money, to others and yourself, too." This is very important to understand, as using your time wisely is paramount, because time is finite and our lives are, too. If we give continually to everyone, with no limit, no boundary, no evaluation of the impact and disregard of our responsibilities and care for ourselves, this is doomed to failure …

Look at yourself honestly and consider all the ways you could give, by assessing your resources and abilities. Giving can be in so many different ways, from giving time, money, guidance, fundraising, love, wisdom and attention. Sometimes the smallest acts and words can have the best effect, as people want to feel uplifted and valued, commendation especially in front of their peers has an immediate positive impact. We must allocate the right amount of time, decide on the right thing to give, consider all our responsibilities, the impact of our giving, and assess the co-operation and the comprehension of the recipient. For example, there is no point advising someone who is so drunk with alcohol or so high on drugs when they are nearly in a comatose state, and trying to give meaningful advice on the misgivings of what they are doing. You need to wait for them to be sober, awake and functioning before you can give in any supportive way.

The Power of Commitment

Commitment is the bridge between my vision (what I want) and reality (what is).

People often underestimate the power of commitment; in fact, without commitment it is very difficult to reach one's objective. A commitment is a pledge that obligates you to a certain course of action. Whatever the topic – whether it is to lead a healthier life, to have a better relationship, or to renew your approach to work – a commitment is one of the most important principles of success.

W. M. Murray, in his book, *The Scottish Himalayan Expedition* (1951), wrote:

"Until one is committed, there is hesitancy, the chance to draw back, always ineffectiveness. Concerning all acts of initiative and creation, there is one elementary truth the ignorance of which kills countless ideas and splendid plans: that the moment one definitely commits oneself, then providence moves, too. All sorts of things occur to help one that would never otherwise have occurred. A whole stream of events issue from the decision, raising in one's favour all manner of unforeseen incidents and meetings and material assistance, which no man could have dreamed would come his way."

Commitment is giving; it is the process of reaching out beyond your limitations and empowering yourself to do whatever is necessary to accomplish a goal. The action of giving is very much part of this process: you must give yourself the opportunity to grow, take risks and expand yourself in life.

Commitment allows the power of the giving process to work towards good causes, using your time, money and knowledge. Revered and respected world leaders are committed to causes which are greater than themselves. Past and present human rights activist leaders engage and show direction through their commitment to a just and fair world. People have a need for their leadership, to guide them in improving their lives or save them from tyranny.

Commitment to relationships is about giving; we must give to receive, and often people approach it the opposite way, expecting to receive before giving. The more committed you are, the more you will want to give and the more chance you have of a successful relationship.

Come Out of Your Comfort Zone

This is a limiting characteristic that many people have, and it is related to "fear". Meaning the fear of the unknown, fear of change, fear of trying something new and not knowing what will happen. These are associated with fear of loss: "What will happen if I do something new? I may lose, be it time, money or opportunity cost." There is also the thought of rejection or not being good enough to try something new; again, they are all related to fear, that little voice at the back of your mind saying you are not good enough.

You cannot achieve your objectives if you cannot come out of your comfort zone; to move forward with what you want to accomplish means you have to enter new situations, meet new people, risk time and/or money without having the certainty of the result.

> *"Fear is not a virtue. It is limiting –
> to live you must transact and interact –
> no boundaries are needed."*

Fear is Limiting – Stops us Giving

Fear plays a big role in many people's lives; it is contagious, it disables people and limits the wonderful moments they could be experiencing. Fear can come in many forms and guises, fear stops people giving to others, stops them giving to themselves opportunities of trying something new outside their comfort zone. Fear of loss is the main factor for people not interacting with others, where they feel it may mean a loss of their time or even money with no guaranteed benefit for themselves. Fear of loss of investing one's knowledge, time and money are all part of the worry that inflicts many. We must allow ourselves the opportunity to live in the knowledge of the unlimited potentials that this world has to offer us, and this can only happen if we let go of the thoughts of fear and go into the unknown territories of life.

The Uncertainty of Life is the Only Certainty

We live in a world where everything is so structured around certainty. There are insurances of all types – health, buildings, contents, travel, business interruption, loss of rent, loan repayment, the list goes on and on. Private pension schemes have proliferated: the worry of old age with no income is something which is ingrained in the adult population of most modern societies. Health and safety has become a major part of every industry; with regulations enforceable by local and central governments on companies and individuals, these sometimes go beyond what is logical.

Having objectives and planning for the future are very important aspects of a successful life; however, this must not take away from living the moment, going with the flow of your feelings. Give yourself the opportunity and the understanding that life in its true sense is one of constant flux and filled with uncertainty. Live and embrace this uncertainty and move with it to experience every moment life has to offer.

Acceptance

We have a real challenge to accept things around us. Acceptance of others who are different, whether physical, age, sex, religion, political beliefs, dress code, living habits, and all sort of other differences. People do not want to accept the circumstances around them: bad weather, death, financial loss, mental illness, dementia, kids' misbehaviour, and many other situations which are not pleasant.

However, this does not mean we should accept injustice, nor does it mean sitting idly and not working towards our objectives. Acceptance is allowing oneself to see everything objectively without letting it affect you, seeing the person and situation as it really is, and not how you interpret or judge it.

Through acceptance comes calm and a break-down of perceived fears, because you are letting go of control and a desire for security. If you suffer from Arachnophobia, you are saying to yourself the spider is there and has a right to live, too; the new person I will meet today may have differing views, but I will accept our differences and perhaps I can also learn something from them. Acceptance creates relief and non-confrontation, and enables a cohesive society, which allows all to work together.

Acceptance is the same as non-judgement. Look at all the wars and conflicts that have come from judging others as being different and wrong, so therefore must be attacked and changed: what good has war done us, except death and destruction?

It is core to our well-being that we accept all around us in our desire to live a life without fear and full of abundance and joy.

Do Not Try to Control

Why do we need to control? We link our security to controlling things around us, we try to control because we fear without control we are weak and this will lead to unhappiness; however, the total opposite is true. If you observe kids, they have boundless energy and are certainly a lot happier than adults – they are not trying to consciously control anything. When you meet people such as monks or priests who have given up all material possessions and any claim for any status in life, they are free and in an exalted state; whatever you may say to them, even derogatory, will not upset them in any way.

Our aim to control and the limiting effect of fear are very much linked.

"Self-preservation and constant desire to expand: these are two instincts – are you here to experience life or avoid it?"

Give Hope and Love

Giving hope and love are powerful tools; these two interconnecting elements of giving can transform people's lives as well as your own, the giver. All our actions are based on perception of something or someone, which then affects our emotions; this in turn either lifts us to feel good or makes us feel depressed. Feeling low and depressed is not a state of mind which will ever generate anything positive in your life; in fact, an extension of feeling depressed can lead to extreme actions or even taking our own life through suicide.

To have hope is to want an outcome that makes your life better. It can not only help make a tough present situation more bearable, but also can eventually improve our lives, because envisioning a better future will motivate you to take the steps to make it happen.

Whether we think about it or not, hope is a part of everyone's life. Everyone hopes for something. It's an inherent part of being a human being. Hope helps us define what we want in our futures and is part of the self-narrative about our lives we all have running inside our minds.

What is Hope?

Hope, said Aristotle, is the dream of a waking man.

One can say "hope" is like "to wish", meaning to cherish a desire with anticipation and to want something to happen or be true.

Hope is not the same as optimism. An optimist generally is more hopeful than others. On the other hand, the most pessimistic person you ever meet can still be hopeful about something. Hope is very specific and focused, usually on just one issue.

Hope is Essential

Most people associate hope with a dire situation. People hope to get out of difficult circumstances. That is often when people do find themselves hoping fervently! But hope can also provide the key to making everyday life better. Research has shown that children who grew up in poverty but had success later in life all had one thing in common – hope. Hope involves planning, motivation and determination to get what one hopes for.

One opposite of hope is fear, which is the desire for something not to happen combined with an anticipation of it happening. Inherent in every hope is a fear, and in every fear a hope. Other opposites of hope are hopelessness and despair, which is an agitated form of hopelessness.

In a way, having hope links your past and present to the future. You have a vision for what you hope will happen. Whether it does not, just envisioning it can make you feel better. And if it's something you can somewhat control – like the kids working to get out of poverty – then hope can motivate you to take whatever steps you need to take.

People Have the Potential to Do Great Things – inspire them!

Every student who walks into a classroom as a diamond in the rough is waiting to be polished. Classes should be as interesting as possible to bring out the best in those students. Of course, it doesn't work with every student. But over time, by making material interesting, it will shift people towards becoming more motivated and hard-working. This is true of coaches, leaders and managers everywhere. If you look at research by Benjamin Bloom[1] and his colleagues about what made somebody a world-class tennis player or a world-class musician, or even a mathematician or a scientist of great acclaim, very rarely were those world-class candidates superior early on in their careers. They looked pretty average when they started with them. But what they had in common was a coach, a teacher and a manager who believed in them and set their aspirations very high. That often created a self-fulfilling prophecy, by inspiring them to engage in more deliberate practice and to put in the 10,000 hours that we all know are critical to achieving expertise.

No Hope – Leads to Suicide, the Ultimate Escape

Suicides resulted in 828,000 global deaths in 2015, an increase from 712,000 deaths in 1990. This makes suicide the 10th leading cause of death worldwide. In a given year this is roughly 12 per 100,000 people.[2]

Deaths: 793,000 / 1.4% of all deaths (2016)

How to Give Hope

We must use best endeavours with the time and resources at our disposal to give hope to all around us, particularly the people who are desperate with mental and physical sickness. Here is how:
- Champion the good you see in them.
- Applaud their achievements however small these may seem to be.
- Praise them about the positive aspects of their character.
- Encourage them to apply their gifts and talents by serving others in the community.
- Let them know they're worth loving.
- Ask for their help or advice if you're working on something they have a passion for, this will increase their self-worth and self-value.

How Do You Keep Hope?

- Remember that every situation has a lesson to learn from. Be philosophical.
- Recall any setbacks in the past. This cannot be the first time you're experiencing bad times.
- Find ways to laugh.
- If you cannot change something, accept it.
- Choose happiness over the right thing.
- Cultivate optimism
- Look at the possibilities in your life, not the limitations
- Look for hope in unexpected places
- Practice gratitude
- Accept all the support you can get.

Give Unconditional Love

Unconditional love means accepting another person for who they are, with all their faults and weaknesses.

Here is how you can make unconditional love part of your life:

Spend time bonding. One of the most important ways to love people is to spend time with them. The time you spend together will help you to understand each other more and to be comfortable around each other. This will create a trusting bond that reinforces your love.

Accept your people for who they are. The people in your life may or may not have values and habits that are similar to your own. Even if you disagree with them, you have to accept them for who they really are. Avoid criticising or trying to change them. Instead, agree to disagree on some things while continuing to love them.

Overlook minor offences. The more time you spend with anyone, the more chances they will have to upset you. If someone does something that bothers you, take some time to decide if it is worth a confrontation. If you decide that it's a minor blunder, just let it pass. If the incident really bothers you, you should talk it over with the other person.

Appreciate others for what they do. If you have people in your life who love you, help you, and support you, try to express to them how grateful you are for their presence in your life. By doing so, they may return the appreciation, building a mutually beneficial relationship of trust and respect.

Get comfortable with affection. When you love people, it is important to give and receive affection. Try to be comfortable with hugging or embracing friends and family members, giving them gifts, and offering them praise. Also, be willing to accept the same things in return.

Express your love. Aside from just giving and receiving affection, you can also be forward about your feelings. You should tell people in your life that you love them and care for them. You also need to allow them to express their feelings to you openly and without judgement or ridicule.

Love is something everyone has a need for, no matter what your background is, be it faith, age, sex or world view. All people have the same need to be accepted and loved. When you give love, you receive love. Love is intertwined with the process of giving and receiving.

Why Should We Give

The Giver

There is gain for the giver. First, giving means we feel a sense of satisfaction having made someone happier and added to their lives in a positive way. Most people whom you give to will value and appreciate your gesture, and they will want to reciprocate in some way. The giver stands out in a group of people; when you give and care for others, they feel uplifted and indebted to the giver. However, your giving has been with no expectation, thereby if nothing is reciprocated you are not disappointed, your continued giving will be daily, weekly, without a timeline and only limited by what you can afford in time or financially – it should be part of your life outlook. Your continued giving will bear fruit, as in most instances people will want to give back, either share with you their knowledge, connections, or want to do business with you. Also, they will give back their care and love, share with you what they have, be happy to see you and embrace you in their warmth of gratitude and human connectivity.

The giver has an enhanced value in other people's eyes: they see the giver as an educator, leader, mentor, motivator, carer, a person that they will turn to when they need help and support, but also the first person to share with, too, and to listen to for direction. Sharing can be personal and professional – if you trust someone as an unconditional giver, you will, at the first chance of sharing a business or professional opportunity, go to them; if they are already in that space, why would you go to someone else who you do not know or trust?

Being a giver has an elevated status in society. Look at all the leaders who have given to others, some even with their lives: Martin Luther King (American Civil Rights Leader), Churchill, Mahatma Gandhi (Indian Civil Rights), Mother Teresa (Roman Catholic nun who devoted her life to serving the poor and destitute around the world), and there are many others.

Giving to Your Family

The happy functional family unit is key to the well-being of people and society. Give of yourself to your family to create harmony and a functional environment for children to grow up in. It is not what we tell our children that matters, it is what we do that they emulate.

We must work at giving to our families unconditionally. Leadership starts at home: we are the leaders to our kids and a role model for their future lives and families.

Teaching Your Children Giving

We must teach children to become caring adults. This can be done by being examples through our own actions, story-telling and mentoring. It's important to reach out and help others who are in need in the presence of children, so they can witness and see what caring is and how it helps the recipient – they can see that giving is a good thing to do. Develop a culture of giving in the home: give kids a small allowance and teach them to save and give a proportion of the money to needy causes; this will allow them to learn a good habit at a young age. Help them to decide to which good cause they would like to give a proportion of their allowance. Remind them that what they are doing is very important and applaud them for their actions.

As kids grow up, they will see the merits of their giving actions; it will give them happiness and they will experience the reciprocation from grateful people. Children who have positive experiences of altruism and generosity in their young lives grow into caring and expansive adults, being both fulfilled in their lives and connected with the world around them.

We must teach kids to have compassion, respect, self-control, empathy, courage and non-discrimination. We are challenged in an interconnected world with so much social media influences, which can have negative effects on our kids. There is no financial reward, or a prize on a stage at the end of bringing up our kids to be successful, upright citizens. Our reward is to see them happy, and living fulfilled lives.

Giving and Understanding Kids

Being a parent is not easy. I know from my own experiences that kids need patience and understanding; they can be very challenging at times. The key is to give them time and understanding; they, like us adults, have their own wants and desires. In their little world, cartoons, sweets and fun things matter, and it's important to understand that.

Adults need to recognise the importance of listening to children so that children know that what they think and feel is valued. If children can begin to understand some of their own feelings, they can grow up balanced and help others to do the same.

Stories can help children to understand their own feelings and the feelings of other children. This is also a very good way to teach kids the difference between right and wrong and how to respect others and think about sharing.

How to Help Kids Learn to Love Giving

Research suggests that kids have a deeply rooted instinct to share and to help others, from the time they're very young – one study even found that toddlers enjoy giving to others more than they like getting treats for themselves. Kids, it seems, have a strong, natural drive to be kind and generous.

Helping kids experience the happiness that comes from giving to others is probably one of the most valuable ways we can nurture generosity in them. Giving makes people happy and happiness promotes giving.

We need to teach and make sure that giving feels good for kids and launches this "positive cycle" of happiness and generosity.

How to teach kids to give and be generous to others is outlined below.

Be a role model and explain why you do what you do – Research has found that kids are more likely to be kind and generous when they have at least one parent who models that behaviour for them.[4]

Help them see the impact – A significant finding from studies of adults is that they'll derive greater happiness from their generosity – and thus be more motivated to give again – if they're able to see the impact it has on others, this is exactly the same for kids.

Help them understand the need to give – For kids to feel compelled to help others, first they have to recognise that their help is actually needed.

Make it part of who they are – Parents want to facilitate their kids' generosity by making donations on their behalf; however, it will be more effective in the long run for kids to have some skin in the game. Kids need to have a part in the giving process, either a proportion of their pocket money, an old toy or doll.

Give them choice – Studies[5] have found that people feel happier after performing kind, helpful and "pro-social" acts only when those acts are voluntary and self-directed;

however, when they feel pressured to help, they feel worse. It is important to present options to kids and give them choices. You need to involve kids in the conversation; otherwise, they feel like it's being forced on them.

What we need is not obedience, we need brilliance – we should use a child to learn, not to just teach.

What Are the Benefits of Giving?

There are many benefits from giving and living in an all-embracing sharing society; in fact, it is our saviour – without giving and sharing, we have a failed state in respect of inner happiness and well-being.

This can be seen by the rise of alcoholism and illegal drug use in societies which are emotionally restrained and non-sharing.

For example, 70,237 drug overdose deaths occurred in the United States in 2017.[6] The age-adjusted rate of overdose deaths increased significantly by 9.6% from 2016 (19.8 per 100,000) to 2017 (21.7 per 100,000). Opioids – mainly synthetic opioids (other than methadone) – are currently the main driver of drug-overdose deaths. Opioids were involved in 47,600 overdose deaths in 2017 (67.8% of all drug overdose deaths).

Giving brings people together, it enhances the quality of their lives, it increases their levels of happiness, it materially affects their lives in a positive way; the giver and the recipient are both better off by their common goal of togetherness. The school of thought of "close your door and mind your own business" is broken and unfulfilling in every respect; it leads to loneliness and depression, and suicide rates are far higher in materialistic, single and individual-orientated societies. Unfortunately, the thought process where someone on meeting a person is thinking "What is in it for me?" is completely non-performing emotionally and materially – we should be thinking, "Who is the other person and what can we do together; how can we enhance one another's lives?"

"I shall pass through this world but once. Any good therefore that I can do or any kindness that I can show to any human being, let me do it now. Let me not defer or neglect it, for I shall not pass this way again"

– Stephen Grellet

Why Giving Makes You Happy

It's proven that …
- People who perform random acts of kindness are significantly happier than those who don't.
- Spending money on others makes you happier than spending money on yourself.
- It's a continual cycle: happier people help others more, which makes them feel good and want to give more, so they give more, and that makes them happier.

- You don't need to donate money to boost your mood – giving your time works just as well.

To give, do the following:
- Give your time to someone else; share your professional hints and tips; help a neighbour; donate your time to a local cause.
- Send a grateful message; gratitude is a powerful emotion that helps us appreciate what we have. Send an email, text or note to someone who has helped you in some way this year. Thank them for what they have done for you, however small.
- Be grateful for three great things that happened today. At the end of today, before you go to sleep, spend a few minutes thinking about three good things that happened today. They don't have to be that remarkable; just three things that made you feel a little better. Repeat as often as you can.
- It is one of life's paradoxes that we limit the power of our giving by having an expectation of getting something in return. The wonderful surprise is that when we give without any thought or desire for something back, our returns can be truly limitless.
- **Give from the heart.** If we truly want to be generous, then we have to give just because we want to give, not because we have ulterior motives and want something in return.

- **Know that being generous will make us happier.** Being generous helps us feel more compassionate towards others, gives a stronger sense of community, and establishes a higher self-image.
- **Notice what would make someone's life easier.** When we talk to someone, start wondering about how we could help them, instead of always thinking about how they can help us.
- **Be grateful for what you have.** Being more grateful will put us in the mindset to be a more generous person. If we are able to appreciate all that we have, we'll be more likely to share some of those great things with others, to help them appreciate life as well.
- **Don't forget to be generous to yourself.** Though volunteering, caring for others, and giving our time is a great way to be generous, we shouldn't forget about yourself completely in the process.

"Keep your mind life-friendly – if you do not handle it properly it will turn into your enemy – everyone can give up on you ultimately."

What to Give

- Share your knowledge.
- Give blood.
- Give recognition.
- Give a helping hand.
- Give a recommendation.
- Give Others Your Respect
- Make someone laugh.
- Give others your care.
- Give good advice.
- Give hope.
- Give love.
- Give encouragement.
- Give money.
- Give your time to listen to others.
- Perform acts of kindness.
- Introductions to other people.
- Give emotional support.
- Give guidance.

*"We make a living by what we get.
We make a life by what we give"*

— Winston S. Churchill

What is the Power of Giving?

"If you want happiness for an hour, take a nap. If you want happiness for a day, go fishing. If you want happiness for a year, inherit a fortune. If you want happiness for a lifetime, help somebody."

– **Chinese proverb**

Today, scientific research provides compelling data to support the notion that giving one's time, talents and treasures is a powerful pathway to finding purpose, transcending difficulties, and finding fulfilment and meaning in life.[7]

There is a growing body of evidence that shows we are evolving to become more compassionate and collaborative in our quest to survive and thrive.

Altruism: The Miracle Drug

The idea of altruism behaving like a miracle drug has been around for at least two decades. The euphoric feeling we experience when we help others is what researchers call the "helper's high", a term first introduced 20 years ago by volunteerism and wellness expert Allan Luks to explain the powerful physical sensation associated with helping others.

In a 1988 piece for *Psychology Today*,[8] Luks looked at the physical effects of giving experienced by more than 1,700 women who volunteered regularly. The studies demonstrated that a full 50 percent of helpers reported feeling "high" when they helped others, while 43 percent felt stronger and more energetic.

As Harvard cardiologist Herbert Benson puts it,[9] helping others is a door through which one can go to forget oneself and experience our natural hard-wired physical sensation. As the runner's high happens when their endorphin levels rise, the helper's high happens when people perform good deeds for others. In other words, the helper's high is a classic example of nature's built-in reward system for those who help others.

But are there rewards, as well, when the act of helping is required and not voluntary?

A 2007 study by economists Bill Harbaugh and Daniel Burghart and psychologist Ulrich Mayr,[10] all from the University of Oregon, explored the differences in brain activity when donations were voluntary or mandatory. They gave each subject $100 and told them that nobody would know how much of it they chose to keep or give away, not even the researchers who enlisted them in the experiment and scanned their brains. Pay-offs were recorded on a portable memory drive that the subjects took to a lab assistant, who then paid the subjects in cash and mailed donations to charity without knowing who had given what.

The brain responses were measured by an fMRI as a series of transactions occurred. Sometimes the subjects had to choose whether to donate some of their cash to a local food bank. Sometimes a tax was levied that sent their money to the food bank without their approval. Sometimes they received extra money, and sometimes the food bank received money without any of it coming from them.

Sure enough, when the typical subject chose to donate to the food bank, he was rewarded with that "warm glow". The areas of the brain that release the pleasure chemical dopamine unexpectedly lit up (the caudate, nucleus accumbent and insula) – the same areas that respond when you eat a dessert or receive money.

Surprisingly, when the subject was forced to pay a tax to the food bank, these pleasure centres were also activated – albeit not as much. Consistent with pure altruism, the experiment found that even mandatory, tax-like transfers to a charity elicit neural activity in areas linked to reward processing. Even when it was mandatory for subjects to donate, the pleasurable response persisted, though it wasn't as strong as when people got to choose whether or not to donate.

"How much of life you capture will determine the significance and quality of your life."

Giving Has Immense Personal Benefits

As stated earlier, giving does not necessarily mean giving out money or material items. People give not because they have but because they have that inherent urge to give. In fact, many well-known philanthropists did not start their charity work when they got rich. They probably didn't know that they would become rich, even when they started charitable work. Even without any material gift to offer, sharing your ideas can have immense personal benefits. Ideas can transform others greatly. Many great things that have been achieved in the world emanated from simple ideas. The benefit of sharing your ideas is that the effect will somehow boomerang back to you. By listening to your own ideas repeatedly as you share with others, you may eventually be inclined to put them in practice yourself, with wonderful results. You will be unlocking your own potential of self-fulfilment. It may eventually seem like a miracle, but that is how selfless giving works.

By giving out what you have without expecting anything in return, you start living a meaningful life. You get to realise your true calling in a life and world full of challenges. If you find meaning in the lives of those in need and do something about it, you will also find meaning in your own life. You find yourself in better health and peace and you achieve more happiness. That is the magic of selfless giving.

"You give but little when you give of your possessions. It is when you give of yourself that you truly give"

– Kahlil Gibran

Quotes About the Power of Giving

"I've learned that you shouldn't go through life with a catcher's mitt on both hands. You need to be able to throw something back."

– Maya Angelou

"Attention is the rarest and purest form of generosity"

– Simone Weil

"The best way to find yourself is to lose yourself in the service of others"

– Mahatma Gandhi

"Anyone who thinks that they are too small to make a difference has never tried to fall asleep with a mosquito in the room"

– Christine Todd Whitman

"If you wait until you can do everything for everybody, instead of something for somebody, you'll end up not doing nothing for nobody"

– Malcolm Bane

"Generosity is the best investment"

– Diane Von Furstenberg

"Never believe that a few caring people can't change the world. For, indeed, that's all who ever have"

– Margaret Mead

"Wherever you are, be all there"

– Jim Elliot

"As we work to create light for others, we naturally light our own way"

– Mary Anne Radmacher

"Never suppress a generous thought"

– Camilla E. Kimball

"Make generosity part of your growth strategy"

– Danielle LaPorte

> *"Act as if what you do makes a difference. It does"*
>
> **– William James**

> *"You can give without loving, but you cannot love without giving"*
>
> **– Victor Hugo**

Cycle of Giving

By setting the example of being the Giver, you become the catalyst for the giving process to grow by creating in people who receive from you the inspiration to give to others. Our world becomes a better place with the flow of giving and sharing touching us all.

The Power of Generosity

Generosity is the virtue of giving good things to others freely and abundantly. The act of generously giving automatically creates reciprocation by those who have received. It is a win-win. By spending our time for the betterment of others' well-being, we enhance our own standing. In letting go of some of what we own, we better secure our own lives. Generosity is a learned character trait that involves having an attitude to giving and practising giving liberally. People who live life generously also tend to enjoy well-being in life. The more generous people are, the more happiness, health, and purpose in life they enjoy. Money cannot buy you happiness, as people rightly say. However, money and happiness are still related, as generous financial givers are happier people, and so whilst money cannot buy you happiness, giving it away actually associates with greater happiness.

Generosity generates its power from the gesture of letting go. Being able to give to others shows us our ability to let go of attachments that otherwise can limit our beliefs and our experiences. It might be in our nature to think, *"That object is mine for whatever reason."* But that thought can simply dissolve. This doesn't just happen passively; we choose to let it through the cultivation of generosity. It is in that choice to dissolve that we carry ourselves to a state of greater freedom.

Our attachments might want to put a cap on our generosity and say, "I will give this much and no more," or "I will give this article or object if I am appreciated enough for this act of giving." But it is through the practice of generosity that we learn to see through the attachments, and create space for ourselves. Being able to step outside of oneself and give is an essential ingredient for happiness. Love and generosity create an exchange of positive energy, and fuel further love and generosity. Nourishing generosity emerges when we give without the need for our offering to be received in a certain way, perhaps wishing to be recognised or validated, but not needing it. When generosity lets go of these kinds of expectations, it is a movement towards freedom.

I have been fortunate to be the recipient of many generous acts by people in my life, and these moments have made me feel loved and cared for. Generosity is the same as love: through generous giving a person is showing love towards the recipient.

One of my most memorable experiences was when I visited Cairo, Egypt, many years ago. A friend, who was a singer I had met at a music festival in Turkey, invited me to his family home in downtown Cairo. It was a small flat in a poor district of this huge city; he and his family had prepared a feast of food, with such variety and abundance. Most importantly they showed me such love, that I still have not forgotten after 30 years.

Another example is when I took a trip to Kenya, again many years ago. Upon my arrival in this most enchanting country, I booked a three-day safari holiday. Within the trip I met probably one of the most courageous and giving people I have had the good fortune to experience. His name was David, a medical doctor from Israel, who was some years older than me, in his early 40s. He had decided when he was in medical school as a young man that he would dedicate some years of his life for the betterment of others, and this was exactly what he was doing. He left his country and had travelled to West Africa to give two years of his life as a volunteer to fight the illness AIDS. He had to leave his wife, family and his work in Israel to do this charitable work. David told me he did not care for money; in his year at medical school his gifted class members had all gone to the USA to make their fortunes, but he had not. He did not own any property, and his ambition had always been to give to others his services as a medical doctor. Even within our trip, one of our party, a young lady, did not have enough money for a ballooning excursion, so he volunteered and paid for her. He took so many photos of our group – this was before we had mobile phones and digital images – and all of these he collated and sent to me after the trip and always kept in touch. A wonderful, inspiring, caring person, whose love and giving to others created lasting memories in their lives.

Community Giving

When the community disintegrates and people live isolated lives, absorbed within themselves, we are all the poorer for it. We are social animals in need of love, affection and one another; we all have moments when we need the support of our family members, friends, and neighbours.

Community giving is the act of connecting with people in your street, block of flats and neighbourhood, and offering your assistance in any way you can provide. People in return will do the same for you; even if some do not, it does not matter – the mere act of offering your support will make you feel better, you will be recognised in the community as a caring person, in many ways a leadership position. Building a community requires that one takes a risk to invest time and energy. This is a risk some people do not want to take, they feel it will be their loss; this is short-sightedness and narrow-minded. Together embracing one another, we can achieve much more than individually isolating and not mixing; community enhancement is key to societal happiness.

Giving to one's community is especially important when it involves children, because if they suffer, then the greater community will also be affected negatively. Volunteering to mentor deprived and neglected children, will give them the building blocks for a better future. We must help so they live up to their full potential.

Take Responsibility and Own Your Actions

*"If you own this story,
you get to write the ending"*

– Brené Brown

By taking responsibility for your life, you allow yourself to unleash your full potential and remove any hindrance on the way of your journey to success.

The greatest day in our lives is when we take total responsibility for our actions.

What Does it Mean to Take Responsibility for Your Actions?

Essentially, this means acknowledging the role you play in your own life, the good bits and the bad bits. Rather than looking around for someone or something else to blame, you must accept that you are in charge of what is going on.

The five essential elements of responsibility are: honesty, compassion, fairness, accountability, and courage. Being responsible makes your life better. When you do what you have promised, people see you as a responsible and reliable person. ... This boosts your self-esteem and self-worth.

When we are responsible, we don't postpone a task because it makes us uncomfortable, or it is something we really don't want to do. We live up to the promises we make, not just to others, but to ourselves as well.

Being responsible also means we learn to manage our time in order to accomplish our goals, but at the same time we don't take on so much that we become overwhelmed. If we over-extend ourselves, it is not healthy for our recovery and we likely won't live up to our commitments.

We take ownership when we believe that taking action is not someone else's responsibility. You, as an individual, are accountable for the quality and timeliness of an outcome, even when you're working with others. You care about the outcome the same way you would care as an owner of the organisation.

Taking responsibility is the first step to developing a healthy sense of self and that we internalise the idea of taking responsibility when we realise, "no one is coming."

It's a liberating concept. Help is not coming. The responsibility is yours, and it starts with developing a belief or habit of mind that you, as an individual, are accountable for the quality and timeliness of an outcome, even when you're working with others. It doesn't always mean you have authority over a project. Nor does it mean that you shouldn't involve others. But it does mean you own the obligation to act and deliver results.

There's a big difference between fault and responsibility. A leader may be responsible for a situation even if it's not his fault. The blame doesn't matter.

Often, we have to deal with situations for which we're not at fault. But fault is backward-looking, and responsibility is forward-looking. Fixating on blame delays taking corrective action and inhibits learning. Focusing on responsibility offers a sense of peace.

In a world where problems are getting more complex, determined and innovative problem-solving will flow from those who live as if help is not coming. Living with responsibility can make us stronger and more action-oriented individuals. It's up to you to make change and take responsibility for outcomes in your professional and personal life.

Happiness is a Choice

No one makes you feel "happy" or "angry"; it's based on how you're interpreting each situation in your life and the meaning you associate to it.

We Can't Ignore Our Emotions

Productivity systems rarely take emotions into account, and feelings are a fundamental and unavoidable part of why humans do what they do.

We can't ignore our emotions.[11] Because of the way our brains are structured, when thought and feelings compete, feelings almost always win. We can't fight our feelings. Research shows this just makes them stronger.

Once you have decided on doing something, made your "To Do" list, you need to boost your emotions up and get things done! Here are the steps:

1. Happiness makes us successful – We become more successful when we are happier and more positive. Optimistic sales people outsell their pessimistic counterparts by 56 per cent. Students primed to feel happy before taking maths achievement tests far outperform their neutral peers. Our brains are literally hardwired to perform at their best not when they are negative or even neutral, but when they are positive.

2. Be Positive – When do we delay or postpone action. Answer: when we're in a bad mood. It's optimism. Happiness increases productivity and makes you more successful.

So how do you get optimistic if you're not feeling it? Monitor the progress you're making and celebrate it. Use small wins to ignite joy and engagement. This pattern is called the progress principle – positive events that influence inner work life: the single most powerful is progress in meaningful work, and of all the negative events, the single most powerful is the opposite of progress – setbacks in the work. Facilitating progress is the most effective way to influence inner work life.

3. Being Rewarded – Research shows that rewards are responsible for three-quarters of why you do things.[12] Perceived self-interest, the rewards one believes are at stake, is a significant reason for predicting dedication and satisfaction towards work. So, treat yourself whenever you complete something on your to-do list.

4. Peer Pressure – Surround yourself with people you want to be and this will make things easier for your self-growth. When people join groups where change seems possible, the potential for that change to occur becomes more real. The groups you associate with often determine the type of person you become. Take education as an example. Why do parents choose their kid's schools? Because they want their offspring to be with kids from certain backgrounds, as well as themselves making friends with the parents. If you're in a group of people who have really high goals for themselves, you'll take on that same sense of seriousness.

Quotes from Celebrated People about Responsibility

"When you hold your baby in your arms the first time, and you think of all the things you can say and do to influence him, it's a tremendous responsibility. What you do with him can influence not only him, but everyone he meets, and not for a day or a month or a year, but for time and eternity"

– Rose Kennedy

"When you think everything is someone else's fault, you will suffer a lot. When you realise that everything springs only from yourself, you will learn both peace and joy"

– Dalai Lama

"The moment you take responsibility for everything in your life is the moment you can change anything in your life"

– Hal Elrod

"Action springs not from thought, but from a readiness for responsibility"

– G. M. Trevelyan

"When you start to accept responsibility for the results you get in life, you also take back the power to change your future outcome"

– Kevin Ngo

"The secret ingredients to true happiness? Decisive optimism and personal responsibility"

– Amy Leigh Mercree

"Making someone responsible for your misery also makes them responsible for your happiness. Why give that power to anyone but yourself?"

– Scott Stabile

"There is an expiry date on blaming your parents for steering you in the wrong direction; the moment you are old enough to take the wheel, responsibility lies with you"

– J.K. Rowling

"Stop blaming other people for your own behaviour! Own the truth. If you don't like it, then invest the time and energy to change it"

– Akiroq Brost

"Blame is the coward's solution to his fear of accountability"

– Craig D. Lounsbrough

"The power behind taking responsibility for your actions lies in putting an end to negative thought patterns. You no longer dwell on what went wrong or focus on whom you are going to blame. You don't waste time building roadblocks to your success. Instead, you are set free and can now focus on succeeding"

– Lorii Myers

"Stop pointing fingers and placing blame on others. Your life can only change to the degree that you accept responsibility for it"

– Steve Maraboli

"You must take personal responsibility. You cannot change the circumstance, the seasons, or the wind, but you can change yourself. That is something you have charge of"

– Jim Rohn

"In the long run, we shape our lives, and we shape ourselves. The process never ends until we die. And the choices we make are ultimately our own responsibility"

– Eleanor Roosevelt

"Take responsibility for your own greatness; no one can take that courage walk for you"

– January Donovan

Asking Can Be Giving

What may surprise you is that asking someone for advice or support can be a way of giving, as it allows someone the opportunity to be a giver, and makes them happy and important, too.

How does giving work within the business and professional world?

When you mention giving to anyone, they automatically think of charity, a loss of their time, money and whatever else they might be giving. In Western societies, and to a greater extent in the whole world, we live with a need for gain, we must take, and only do something if we see a direct reward; hence, this is linked to expectation. Expectation is one of our greatest curses; it ultimately creates unhappiness, where we always reach a point when one or more of our expectations are not met and this leads to disappointment and sadness.

Our best decisions are made when we are calm and peaceful within ourselves; when we have no inner turmoil, we blossom as people, and our decisions are not based on fear or insecurities but through wisdom and clarity of thought.

Professional and business success comes from investing. An investment can be time and money. Giving should be looked upon as being part of the investment process, but without necessarily any expectation.

You decide on your professional objectives: where you want to reach and when you expect to reach the place you want to be, and this means you establish a timeline. Your objectives will always involve people; they can be clients, business partners, employers, employees, service providers, advisors, suppliers, investors and lenders. You need to impact these people in such a way that they will want to do business with you. What better way than to give to them without any expectations? This can be in positive uplifting communications, advice and guidance on the subject that you specialise in, even personal offers of assistance, care and support. When someone sees you giving without expectation, your credibility will rise in their eyes, as will their trust levels, and you will certainly stand out in front of masses who are only thinking about what they can receive without ever considering what they can give.

In my business activities, when I meet a potential business partner, I will offer help and assistance irrespective of whether we do business or not; in essence, this makes me feel good just to help and advise with no expectation – but it also creates a positive bond with the receiving party.

'Giving' and putting others first is a trait of many top performers – across a whole spectrum of fields, including business and politics. However, some 'givers' also underperform – those who sacrifice their own needs and goals too much.

'Takers', on the other hand (those who put themselves first), may get better results in the short-term, but are more likely to be 'middle of the road' performers over the longer term. Cuddled between 'givers' above and below them on the success ladder.

So, while coming from a place of wanting to do what's best for others may slow down your journey to success, it could also be more rewarding, make a difference to more people and yield more business success over the longer term.

Within organisations, encourage a culture of where seeking help is the norm, and successful givers recognise it's okay to receive. In surveys, between 75% and 90% of respondents confirmed that giving starts with a request; however, most people are shy to ask in a culture where giving is not prevalent.

When vetting and interviewing new staff and throughout their trial work period, it's important to be on the lookout for takers; do not let them into your organisation, weed them out. Takers will negatively impact the morale of the givers within the team; they are great at kissing up and kicking down. Allow a giver into an organisation and you will witness the explosion of generosity within the team members.

I encourage you to consider how you could 'give' to build your business, in a way that makes a difference to others and gets your own needs met, too …

"It takes a noble man to plant a seed for a tree that will some day give shade to people he may never meet"

– **D. Elton Trueblood**

Most Successful Leaders Are Givers

Is it hard for a top leader to be a giver? Because by concentrating on the specific needs of a few, he risks letting down the many.

First, leaders should multiply themselves and create networks of givers. To build cultures where this becomes the norm and, as a result, to be able to delegate a lot of the giving to people around and below them. That provides an opportunity to spread their giving farther than people who are not at the top.

You model it, and that produces legions of matchers who find the best way to pay it back is to pay it forward. Leaders encourage their first groups of mentees to mentor people below them and start these pay-it-forward chains. You are role modelling and delegating to your mentees to spread the word and become role models themselves. We need good leaders; be they political, business, social, family or parental, the role models play a vital part in how the world moves forward.

How do you balance the desire to be a giver with the need to make tough decisions?

It can be difficult, especially for the agreeable givers who really care about being nice and polite. Givers in leadership roles must draw a sharp distinction between being liked and being respected. You don't want to wander around thinking that being a giver means everybody loves you. Then you end up being this insufferable people-pleaser who never makes the right or the tough decisions. Being respected is about doing what is right for the organisation or the group as opposed to the individual or certain constituents.

Looking Out for the Greatest Good

It is often hard for givers to do lay-offs and to make unpopular decisions. But there are a lot of givers who are able to make those decisions precisely because they are looking out for the greatest good. The interest of the majority must be kept in mind.

"Is this where I can have the greatest impact?" I think that's a critical question for a leader. If you spend your time speaking and giving to everyone, you will not be able to do the greatest good. Time is finite, and it must be used wisely; that does not mean you only give where there are big results – it means giving where you can, but not to the detriment of the greater good.

It's important to design jobs where people get to see their end users.

There is a huge difference between "receiving" and "taking". Taking is trying to claim value from people with very self-serving intentions and very little willingness to pay it backward or forward. Receiving is what makes the giving side of an exchange work. There are people willing to accept the contributions of others and either respond with gratitude and appreciation or try to model that in future interactions, when they are in the position to give.

People are pretty good at seeing the self-serving motives behind façades of generosity. Sometimes, fakers get away with it for the short run, but not the long run. Anyway, trying to fake generosity is more work than living it; people tend to see through the motives. You leave a very transactional feeling when you help somebody to get something in return, as opposed to trying to use your knowledge, skills, and connections to benefit other people when you can.

Communications is a Powerful Tool in Giving

Communicating is a very powerful tool in your armoury of giving. Words matter a lot, and what you say, when you say it, and to whom you say it, can have a tremendous effect on the recipient, particularly if it is authentic and you mean what you say.

In my daily life I go out of my way to recognise when something is done well to commend people, and this starts from my own family, my wife and my young kids. I also do the same with friends; it's important to emotionally lift the closest people around you, to energise them with positive and constructive words. This is the same with strangers; everybody wants to feel good about themselves, in a world where many are unhappy in their lives. The unhappiness could be related to their job, income, their looks, age, loneliness, basically feeling not good in themselves, so your encouraging words can have a tremendous positive affect.

I have many examples, I will share a recent one, this occurred over Christmas 2020 when I was on holiday in Bahrain with my family.

We booked into an elegant 262 room hotel on the coast, just outside Manana, the capital of Bahrain. The most important aspect of this hotel was the service – it was excellent right from the chamber-maid to the General Manager.

I made it my business from the moment I realised how great the customer care was to compliment and positively impact all the staff I came in contact with. The head waiter, who looked after our table every breakfast and dinner, gave us excellent and professional service. I made sure the Restaurant Manager was informed about the head waiter's performance, who was also excellent in the way he carried out his managerial responsibilities. The Director of Food and Beverages was also notified of the great team he had, and upon hearing this he came to meet me. I asked to be connected with the General Manager of the hotel, to whom I was duly introduced. The same positive message was given to the GM, but within these communications others were also mentioned, such as the guest relations manager and the hotel security.

The result of the above was the satisfaction of the staff for having been recognised and commended for their efforts. We were treated as if we were royalty at this hotel, with absolute care and kindness, and we were upgraded to one of the best rooms and were presented gifts. I spent no more money than I had budgeted and the staff actions towards us were not to do with any big tips, they were purely to do with my words of encouragement.

Therefore, always commend people when they give their best – the benefits will come back to you in many ways, and you will feel uplifted by their gratitude.

Public Speaking and Giving

We can reach out to a single individual when we are giving our guidance and knowledge; however, we can connect with tens, hundreds and even thousands of people in one session if we are publicly speaking. The public speaker's job is to give to their audience, not take away. Most effective sales people put themselves into their audiences' or clients' place and talk from the listeners' perspective.

Public speaking is probably the most effective way to influence large numbers in a positive and impactful way. I would add the internet is second, because as we know the modern-day mass communication tool is online; however, this is can only be second to a real-life experience of hearing and seeing someone in front of you or on stage.

Public Speeches that had a Profound Effect in History

"The Gettysburg Address"
– Abraham Lincoln, 1863

The American President delivered this now-iconic speech on a battlefield in Pennsylvania during the Civil War, following the Battle of Gettysburg and marking the dedication of the Gettysburg National Cemetery. Though it was not scheduled to be the main address of the day, this brief, 272-word speech has become one of the most enduring in American history.

"Freedom or Death"
– **Emmeline Pankhurst, 1913**

Delivered by British activist Emmeline Pankhurst in Hartford, Connecticut, this address brought together suffragists and suffragettes from both nations, joined in the battle for voting rights. In it, she described herself as a soldier in a civil war waged by women, and she underscored the fact that while male revolutionaries had long been heard and understood, women had been overlooked and cast aside.

During the speech, Pankhurst also addressed her sometimes controversial use of militant methods, comparing them with the Boston Tea Party during the American Revolution. She passionately spoke about the injustice of denying the vote to half of the population, whether in the United States or her homeland.

"We Shall Fight on the Beaches"

– **Winston Churchill, 1940**

The British Prime Minister delivered this speech, one of several historic addresses during the Second World War, to the House of Commons on 4th June, 1940, following the Battle of Dunkirk. With the threat of a Nazi invasion looming – along with the possible fall of France – Churchill made the promise to fight, alone if need be, and to never surrender his nation.

The speech – and the iconic lines, "We shall fight on the beaches, we shall fight on the landing grounds, we shall fight in the fields and in the streets, we shall fight in the hills" – was addressed, in part, to the British as a show of strength amid painful and demoralising circumstances. However, it should also be read as an appeal to the United States to join the fight against Nazi Germany.

"I Have a Dream"

– Dr Martin Luther King Jr, 1963

This historic speech from the American civil rights activist Dr King, made a hundred years after the "Gettysburg Address" and the emancipation of enslaved people in the United States, brought into focus the injustices of racial segregation, inequality, discrimination, and police brutality. It was delivered on a sweltering hot summer day, and 250,000 people, having travelled from around the country, were in attendance.

Dr King drew inspiration from the Bible, history, literature, and music. Perhaps the most famous line – and the one from which the speech gets its name – was inspired midway through the address when the singer Mahalia Jackson cried out from the stands, "Tell 'em about the 'Dream',

Martin, tell 'em about the 'Dream'!" It was a reference to earlier speeches, and Dr King understood immediately, setting aside the prepared words and improvising some of the most important words in American history.

"I Am Prepared to Die"
– Nelson Mandela, 1964

During the proceedings at the Rivonia Trial, the anti-apartheid revolutionary and political leader Nelson Mandela delivered this three-hour speech from the defendant's dock in lieu of testifying, addressing the charges he faced and the realities of apartheid in South Africa. At the time, he was accused of sabotage, and, if convicted, he could face the death penalty.

In those pivotal three hours, addressing the judge in a segregated courtroom, Mandela spoke about the exploitation and oppression of Black people in South Africa. He discussed the many ways in which the struggle for equality had (thus far) been blocked by legislation and government violence. He also laid bare the injustices of poverty and alluded to the fundamental human right to live in dignity.

Givers and Takers

Takers

The takers are people who, when they walk into an interaction with another person, are trying to get as much as possible from that person and contribute as little as they can in return, thinking that's the shortest and most direct path to achieving their own goals. This ultimately has limited success as there are few people who are gullible twice, as well if you wish to work with smart established people they will see through the façade and will stop giving after an initial period of openness, because oftentimes, takers burn bridges.

Givers

It's not just about donating money or volunteering necessarily, but looking to help others by making an introduction, giving advice, providing mentoring or sharing knowledge, without any strings attached. These givers actually prefer to be on the contributing end of an interaction. The act of giving makes them feel satisfied in the knowledge that they have made a positive impact on other people's lives.

Matchers

Most people hover somewhere in between giving and taking. These people are matchers.

A matcher is somebody who tries to maintain an even balance of give and take. If I help you, I expect you to help me in return. They keep score of exchanges, so that everything is fair and really just.

Who are Achieving the Most?

One would think that it must be the matchers who are more generous than takers, but also protect their own interests, who would rise up to the top the quickest. However, research and data has shown that the givers are over-represented at the top.[13]

In sales, the most productive sales people are actually those who put their customers' interests first. A lot of that comes from the trust and the goodwill that they have built, but also the reputations that they create.

The success of givers and the fall of takers is also driven by matchers. A matcher believes in a just world. A taker violates that belief in a just world. Matchers cannot stand to see takers get ahead by taking advantage of other people. The data on this suggests that matchers will often go around trying to punish them, often by gossiping and spreading negative reputational information.

Just as matchers hate seeing takers get away with exploitation, they also hate to see people act really generously and not get rewarded for it. Matchers will go out of their way to promote and help and support givers, to make sure they actually do get rewarded for their generosity. That's one of the most powerful dynamics behind the rise of givers.

Oftentimes, givers put themselves at risk in the short run. But in the long run, they end up building the kind of social capital that's really important for success in a very connected world. Givers do, in the short run, sometimes lose.

The question you should ask yourself: "Is this person a taker, a giver or a matcher?" Most are not takers, but they are easy to spot; usually it's only one-way traffic with them, asking favours, asking too many questions, never being grateful in any way, so just avoid them.

Givers tend to build broad networks. What givers typically do when they meet somebody new is try to figure out, "How can I add value to this person's life, and what could I possibly contribute that might benefit this person?" What that typically means is they end up creating a lot of goodwill in the relationships that they build that often lies dormant until they may actually need it.[14]

How Do You Spot a Taker?

A study by Chatterjee and Hambrick[15] looked at over 100 computer companies and actually downloaded the annual reports of each.

The aim was to identify the taker CEOs without ever meeting them. They got Wall Street analysts to rate how much each CEO is a taker. These analysts who knew the CEOs and interacted with them, rated the extent to which they were entitled and narcissistic and self-serving.

The first factor that really correlated highly with those ratings was the gap in compensation between the CEO and the next highest-paid executive. Typically, a computer industry CEO makes about two to two and a half times as much annual compensation as the next highest-paid executive in that company. The typical taker CEO had about seven times more annual compensation than the next highest-paid executive in that company. They literally took more in terms of compensation.

The second cue was looking at their speech. The takers tended to use first-person singular pronouns, like "I" and "me", as opposed to "us" and "we", when talking about the company.

The third was that the takers literally felt "it's all about me: I am the most important and central figure in this company". When you looked at their photos in the company's annual reports, they actually had larger photos. They were more likely to be pictured alone.

One of the easiest ways that you can look for a taker is to look for a pattern that translates from Dutch as basically "kissing up, kicking down". Takers tend to be very careful at impression management and ingratiation when they're dealing with someone superior or more influential. But it's hard to keep up the façade in every interaction. It's often peers and subordinates who have a more direct window into what this person's true motives are like.

When Mahatma Gandhi edited a magazine, he would receive all kinds of letters. One letter was from a young woman who was about to get engaged. She was going to meet her prospective fiancé for the first time. She wanted to know how she could judge this person.

The advice Mahatma Gandhi gave her, in the columns of the magazine that he edited, was, "Don't look at how he treats you. Look at how he treats his servants." I think that's very, very telling, because with somebody whom he was trying to impress, obviously he would be very well-behaved. But a true sign of character is how you treat people who are vulnerable.

"The true measure of a man is how he treats someone who can do him absolutely no good"

– **Samuel Johnson**

Giving and Collaboration

If I give you credit for your contributions, that doesn't necessarily take away from my contribution. That makes it a lot easier to keep people on board in a team over time. Here you are allowing your team to shine individually and to be recognised. It means, typically, that if you're a leader or a manager, people will follow you if you rotate to a different organisation or a different job. That's really powerful, but often harder to do.

"If you keep the past alive within you, you will become dead to the present"

– Sadhguru, Indian yogi and author

What Can Givers Do to Avoid Burn-out?

Risks actually can be mitigated with careful strategies. A lot of it comes down to setting boundaries. Many givers confuse being helpful or being generous with being available for every person and every request all the time. There are other givers who confuse being generous with empathising and dropping everything that you're doing to help others. There are also plenty of givers out there who feel like it's uncomfortable or inappropriate to advocate for their own interests. I think that we need to work with people who fall in the giving end of the spectrum to help them set clear boundaries.

Smartness in the Way You Give

"Give in such a way that will take me five minutes or less?" It's basically about finding high benefit to others, but low cost to the self. This fits in with the wider picture of prioritising the giving and multi-tasking.

The takers tend to be purely selfish, while the givers, who are purely selfless, constantly put other people's interests ahead of their own.

But there's this other group of givers that I call "smart givers". They are concerned about benefitting others, but they also keep their own interests at heart, too.

They will look for ways to help others that are either low cost to themselves or even high benefit to themselves, i.e. win-win as opposed to win-lose.

The selfless givers might be more altruistic in principle, because they are constantly elevating other people's interests ahead of the care of themselves. The smart givers are able to sustain their giving by looking for ways that giving can hurt them less or benefit them more.

Selfless givers are at much greater risk of burn-out and exploitation than are smart givers.

"How do I treat most of the people most of the time?" This is the most important consideration.

"What type of giving energises you or is most consistent with your skills?" For some people, it's making introductions. For others, it's sharing credit. For others, it's stepping up as a mentor. Finding your own giver style is really powerful. Your giving must make others better and lift them up, instead of cutting them down.

Givers are others-focused, and tend to provide support to others with no strings attached. They ask themselves, "How can I add value for this person? What can I contribute?"

How to be a Successful Giver

Five-minute favours
Do other people small favours that take no more than five minutes – like making an introduction, giving feedback, and offering advice.

Ask for help
Ask a friend or co-worker for help on an issue you're having, without taking up too much of their time.

While asking for help doesn't sound like a giver move, doing so comes with some surprising benefits. It gives them the opportunity to be a giver, but also makes them feel good and smart.

Specialise in favours
Pick ways of helping that you enjoy and excel at, rather than being a jack of all trades.

This way, you can help in a way that energises you instead of exhausting you. People won't come to you for favours that don't fit these skills.

Be an authentic giver
The key to being a successful giver is also being an authentic giver. The less you try to give to get, the more you'll succeed.

Receiving Is Harder Than Giving

When someone offers a kind word or a present, do you find this difficult to accept or do you allow yourself to deeply receive the gift of kindness, caring, and connection?

Some reasons why receiving is often more difficult than giving:

Defence Against Intimacy – Receiving creates connection. Prioritising giving over receiving may be a way to keep people distant and our hearts defended. To the extent that we fear intimacy, we may disallow ourselves from receiving a gift or compliment, thereby depriving ourselves of a precious moment of connection.

Letting Go of Control – When we give, we're in control in a certain way. It might be easy to offer a kind word or buy someone flowers, but can we allow ourselves to surrender to the good feeling of receiving a gift? And to what extent does our giving actually come from a generous heart versus promoting our self-image of being a caring person?

Receiving Invites Us to Welcome a Vulnerable Part of Ourselves – Living in this tender place, we're more available to receive the gifts we're offered every day, such as a sincere "thank you", a compliment, or a warm smile.

We Believe It Is Selfish to Receive – Our religion may have taught us that we're selfish if we receive, that life is more about suffering than being happy. It's better to be self-effacing and not take up too much space or smile too broadly, lest we bring too much attention to ourselves. As a result of this conditioning, we might feel shame to receive.

A Self-Imposed Pressure to Reciprocate – Blocks to receiving may be a way to protect us from being in someone's debt. We may suspect their motives, wondering, "What do they want from me?" Presuming that compliments or gifts are attempts to control or manipulate us, we pre-emptively defend ourselves from any sense of obligation or indebtedness by not opening ourselves to the gift.

Practice Non-Judgement

The key reason why we have conflict in most cases starts with judging the other to be wrong, for being or thinking differently. The being different could be their sexuality, age, their dress sense, and, most often, it's their colour of skin and religion, and the list of how someone can be different is very long. What we must do is to give to the other the respect and understanding they are due, meaning we must listen to them without judging what they say as wrong; even if it is completely different to our own way of thinking, this does not mean you have to agree.

Through non-judgement you will also open your mind up to learning from others; this means you will have an open mind, not closed, hence increase the potentials in your life to experience more. There are many views about many things in life; these are all that they are, a way of looking at something based on one's past experiences, culture, religion, gender, upbringing, schooling, age, etc. The important perspective for life is to see it as it really is, and this can only be achieved through non-judgement and open-mindedness. Your opinion of right or wrong, good or bad, is from your conditioned mind. This conditioned mind is what we are looking to become free of. Every moment is as it is. Nothing is good or bad, right or wrong, or has any meaning. It is the ego that places these judgements on things.

Non-judgement can be applied to anything – people, situations, thoughts, feelings or things. It takes you deeper into the truth of reality.

"If your attention is on all the time, without any kinds of thoughts or judgements, you will naturally become intuitive"

– Sadhguru

Non-judgement allows for instant inner peace. It means you are instantly still and alert when you choose not to judge. When you experience non-judgement, you will experience freedom.

Laziness and How to Eliminate It

Laziness is an unwillingness to spend energy. It is an unwillingness to do a task we perceive to be difficult or uncomfortable.

For thousands of years, human behaviour has been primarily governed by instant rewards and gratification. Our focus as a human race has for a long time been on immediate returns. Our ancestors had to ensure their survival by constantly searching for food and warding off predators. Today, especially in the first world countries, survival is ensured rather easily. We have a lot of time to be lazy and do nothing – and our survival won't be threatened at all.

Laziness only appeared on the scene of human behaviour with technological advancements. These not only made survival easier, but allowed us to sort of 'plan' for the distant future. Laziness is so prevalent in today's society and seems to have a correlation with the advancements in technology.

To overcome laziness, you need to get into the habit of chasing long-term goals. Then, you need to ensure that your goals are in line with your interests and purpose. Lastly, make sure you're not engaging in self-deception. As far as long-term goals are concerned, if you don't have enough willpower, you can stick to them if you use your evolutionary programming for your own benefit.

This may include making the long-term goal appear nearer by visualisation. Or you can let your reward-hungry brain notice the small, incremental progress that you make on the path of accomplishing your long-term goal.

Whatever you do, the most important thing is to make sure the goal is important enough for you. When you have a strong 'why' to do something, you'll eventually find the 'how'.

Remember that laziness is fundamentally avoidance behaviour. All you're doing is avoiding pain – physical or mental.

Give All At Once

You can devote a particular day or part of a day each week to helping people out.

There are two ways to give: you can do random acts of kindness throughout your week, or put all of your giving acts into one day. Which is most effective? The research shows giving acts into one day leaves you with a bigger psychological boost of feeling appreciation and meaningfulness, which will motivate you to continue being a giver.

How Should You Give?

Pick a couple of ways of helping that you enjoy, rather than being a jack of all trades.

This way, you can help in a way that energises you instead of exhausting you. By specialising in a certain way of giving, it will allow you to gain a reputation as a person with a particular expertise you're willing to share, rather than as a nice person who's freely available. Most people will only come to you for favours that fit your skills and knowledge. The key to being a successful giver is also being an authentic giver. The less you try to give to get, the more you'll succeed.

Caring

The narrow definition of caring is someone that shows kindness and concern for others. A person who is concerned about others and who does kind things for them is an example of someone who would be described as caring.

Caring is a very important and noticeable way to give; it has an immediate effect on the recipient, both emotional and psychologically. The act of caring can be in differing ways, from being a volunteer in a charity to operating a business and caring about your clients and employees. When people know they are cared for, they react in a very different way than if the instruction or communication came from someone who does not care. People listen to others who care about them, and respond positively.

We must first care to be cared back: the mere act of caring will automatically make you feel good. Why is caring so important? Caring means paying attention to detail. Caring is about what you do and make, an effort to do your best. Care about your health and see that you do things that are good for you. When you care, you put in that extra effort to make sure that something works for you or the other person you care about.

Caring in a Business Environment

You may wonder how can caring assist in the business environment, an office, or a business deal? Well, it does help tremendously.

Let's take a business deal. If you care for your business transaction, you will take care to know your deal partner or business contact well. This means you need to know who they are and what they want out of the deal, their angle and objectives. By understanding the other party, you can angle your offer accordingly; the other party will certainly take you more seriously if they see you caring for their interests as well as yours. Most people know what they want – you need to know what the other party wants and bring the two parties' objectives together. There are times this may not be possible; again, caring helps to speed up this process of recognition.

We can take the example of owning and operating a restaurant. This is a people business: the more you care about attention to detail of the food quality, cleanliness, your customers and, most importantly, the staff, the greater your chances of success and sustaining the long term success.

Sharing is Giving

This is what Wikipedia says about sharing: "Sharing is the joint use of a resource or space. It is also the process of dividing and distributing. In its narrow sense, it refers to joint or alternating use of inherently finite goods, such as a common pasture or a shared residence."

However, sharing is also another fundamental way of giving; the act of sharing is literally giving. You can share your knowledge, money, experiences, contact base, guidance, and in many other ways. Sharing immediately creates a bond with others; it has a direct effect on the recipient, and they feel by your sharing act that you are open and accessible.

In modern developed societies, sadly the emphasis is not about a sharing society, it's about individual gain, personal growth, ambition, looking after number one, which is you. We are bombarded by the attributes of individualism and its benefits. Individualistic cultures stress that people should be able to solve problems or accomplish goals on their own without having to rely on assistance from others. This tendency to focus on personal identity and autonomy is a pervasive part of a culture that can have a profound influence on how a society functions. I would add, perhaps makes it dysfunction. One can say individualism is a social pattern that consists of loosely linked individuals who view themselves as independent of collectives, thereby having more control over their lives to do as they wish, and to be in control of their lives. Individualistic societies urge people to pursue personal achievement, which creates competition between individuals, and these systems can also result in high social mobility, which leads to high social anxiety. In addition, the focused attention on personal achievements can bear a significant cost on interpersonal relationships, thereby creating loneliness, depression and unhappiness.

Individualism versus Collectivism

Individualism stresses individual goals and the rights of the individual person. Collectivism focuses on group goals, what is best for the collective group, and personal relationships.

An individualist is motivated by personal rewards and benefits. Individualist persons set personal goals and objectives based on self. Individualistic workers are very comfortable working with autonomy and not as part of a team.

The collectivist is motivated by group goals. Long-term relationships are very important. Collectivistic persons easily sacrifice individual benefit or praise to recognise and honour the team's success. In fact, being singled out and honoured as an individual from the rest of the team may be embarrassing to the collectivistic person.

The generalised geographic clusters of individualism may be found in Anglo countries, Germanic Europe, and Nordic Europe. Geographic clusters for collectivism are often located in Arab countries, Latin America, Confucian Asia, Southern Asia, and Sub-Saharan Africa.

Giving Creates Abundance

Abundance is producing more than you need for yourself so you can begin blessing others with what you have; it could be food, money, love, guidance, knowledge, practically anything that can be a positive in another's life. According to the law of abundance, whatever you give to the world, it will give back to you in some way or another.

It is the innate tendency of nature and of life to manifest, grow, and become more. It is the tendency of the life-force to produce more, and create more, of everything.

Abundance mentality says that there is enough for everyone, so someone else's gain is not your loss. To be grateful for what you have is a key way of creating abundance. This starts from the moment you wake up in the morning, positive and eager to be alive and start your day in the right way.

Be ready for opportunities, open your eyes with eagerness to see what your day will offer you. Capture every opportunity and make it your own, make the most of every opportunity. To capture and create opportunities you will have to connect with credible people, turn these into friendships, and build on these relationships.

The law of abundance basically teaches you to tap into the power of your mind and your beliefs to achieve your dreams. Use positive feeling towards a specific thing, by communicating with kindness, compassion, and goodwill.

Create Unlimited Opportunities

To give means to create unlimited opportunities for yourself through the interaction with others. Giving allows you to experience the true wonder of the world; as situations arise, your attitude of positive and smart giving will mean connections are being created every day. When you meet people, treat them with respect and value, as if it is the last time you will ever see them – imagine the powerful impression you will leave with them: they will not forget the moment they met you.

Life is abundance, and to connect to this abundance we must be open to it. We cannot be open if we walk around being cautious and limited, living in fear of loss, fear of the unknown, limited in giving to ourselves the opportunities we deserve. We must open up and see the wonders that exist: nature, life and the wondrous world we live in.

Produce more ideas than you need for yourself so you can share and give your ideas away. That is called fruitfulness and abundance.

What is abundance and how can you manifest it in your life? Abundance means plenty, or a very large quantity of something. It is the innate tendency of nature and of life to manifest, grow, and become more.

Scientists say that the Universe is always expanding and growing, and even new stars are being created. This is abundance on a cosmic level. Abundance is everywhere in the Universe, and it can also appear in your personal life, if you let it.

People often associate abundance with money. Wealth and having a lot of money is abundance, but abundance manifests in many other ways, not only as plenty of money and possessions.

Abundance is many things, and here are a few of them.
- There is abundance in love.
- There is abundance of friendships.
- There is abundance of opportunities.
- There is abundance of fun.
- There is abundance of food.
- It is possible to have abundance of good deeds.
- It is possible to possess abundance of energy.
- There is abundance of trees, grass or water.
- You can create for yourself abundance of time to do what you want.
- You can also have abundance of spirituality in your life.
- There is abundance of everything on this planet. You may not have access to this abundance, because you alienate yourself from it and prevent it from manifesting in your life.

To attract abundance into your life, you need to feel abundant. You have to develop an "abundance consciousness". "Abundance consciousness" means becoming aware of the existence of abundance, of feeling it in your life, and of connecting with it, even if it doesn't seem to be a part of your life at this moment. This kind of consciousness means feeling and believing that you are a part of it and it is part of your life.

This kind of consciousness-awareness opens your mind to see it around you, and to recognise opportunities. "Abundance consciousness" breaks through the limiting beliefs of your mind and opens your mind to wider opportunities and a wider point of view.

"Giving is the secret of abundance"

– Swami Sivananda

The real key to feeling good is to give and keep on giving, allowing the abundance to flow.

Giving to others is one of life's most rewarding activities. Help those less fortunate than you. Make a difference to their world – and yours!

The power of giving is about you and your potential. You can improve every part of your own life by giving. Giving is a key part of every person's life.

"Receiving is as necessary as giving. To graciously receive is an expression of dignity of giving. Those who are unable to receive are actually incapable of giving. Giving and receiving are different aspects of the flow of energy in the universe"

— **Deepak Chopra**

"Be open to receiving from any source that honours your integrity, and be willing to get what you have asked for ... The more easily you can receive, the more easily the universe can give to you"

— **Sanaya Roman**

Give Meditation Time to Yourself

There are many mental health benefits of meditation;[16] these include better focus and concentration, improved self-awareness and self-esteem, lower levels of stress and anxiety, and it can also foster kindness. There are also benefits for your physical health: it can improve your tolerance for pain and help fight substance addiction.

Meditation has been linked to larger amounts of grey matter in the hippocampus and frontal areas of the brain.[17] Meditation is an exercise for the brain. Through meditation, we can build up areas of our brain and actually rewire it to enhance positive traits like focus and decision-making and diminish the less positive ones like fear and stress. Most importantly, this means there is a possibility to change your brain for the better in a way that is long-lasting.

When you practice mindfulness, you can carry it out to everyday life. Mindfulness helps you to savour life, change habits, live simply and slowly, be present in everything you do.

Seated meditation is the arena in which the meditator practices his own fundamental skills. The game the meditator is playing is the experience of his own life, and the instrument upon which he plays is his own sensory apparatus. Even the most seasoned meditator continues to practice seated meditation, because it tunes and sharpens the basic mental skills he needs for his particular game. We must never forget, however, that seated meditation itself is not the game. It's the practice. The game in which those basic skills are to be applied is the rest of one's experiential existence. Meditation that is not applied to daily living is sterile and limited.

One of the most memorable events in your meditation career is the moment when you first realise that you are meditating in the midst of some perfectly ordinary activity. You are driving down the freeway or carrying out the trash and it just turns on by itself. This unplanned outpouring of the skills you have been so carefully fostering is a genuine joy. It gives you a tiny window on the future. You catch a spontaneous glimpse of what the practice really means. The possibility strikes you that this transformation of consciousness could actually become a permanent feature of your experience. You realise that you could actually spend the rest of your days standing aside from the debilitating clamouring of your own obsessions, no longer frantically hounded by your own needs and greed. You get a tiny taste of what it is like to just stand aside and watch it all flow past. It's a magic moment.

It is important for you to understand what meditation is. It is not a special posture, and it's not just a set of mental exercises. Meditation is a combination of mindfulness and the application of that mindfulness once cultivated. You do not have to sit to meditate; there are many ways to meditate: you can meditate while washing the dishes. You can meditate in the shower, or roller-skating, or typing letters. Meditation is awareness, and it must be applied to each and every activity of one's life.

Carrying your meditation into the events of your daily life is not a simple process. That transition point between the end of your meditation session and the beginning of "real life" is a long jump. It's too long for most of us. We find our calm and concentration evaporating within minutes, leaving us apparently no better off than before. In order to bridge this gulf, Buddhists over the centuries have devised an array of exercises aimed at smoothing the transition. They take that jump and break it down into little steps. Each step can be practised by itself. These are walking meditation, postures, slow-motion activity, breath co-ordination, and concentration on all activities.[18]

Give yourself the opportunity to learn and practice meditation on a daily basis – it will certainly enhance your life.

Mindfulness

Mindfulness is the practice of purposely focusing your attention on the present moment – and accepting it without judgement. Mindfulness also involves acceptance, meaning that we pay attention to our thoughts and feelings without judging them – without believing, for instance, that there's a "right" or "wrong" way to think or feel in a given moment. Mindfulness is scientifically proven to be a key element in stress reduction and overall happiness.[19]

Mindfulness will help you with moments of anger, as anger is often a manifestation of emotions linked to fear, sadness, disappointment. It usually develops in response to the unwanted actions of another person who is perceived to be disrespectful, demeaning, threatening or neglectful. Understanding why you are feeling the way you are feeling can assist in calming yourself, and mindfulness will help heal your anger.

Help Someone

Helping someone else often enables us to forget about ourselves and to feel grateful for what we have. It also feels good when you are able to make a difference for someone else.

Instead of focusing on your own weaknesses, volunteer to mentor, assist or teach another, and you'll see your self-confidence grow automatically in the process.

Gratitude

Be thankful for what you already have and see the miracles that come from this one simple act.

Gratitude helps people refocus on what they have instead of what they lack.

The word gratitude is derived from the Latin word *gratia*, which means grace, graciousness, or gratefulness. Gratitude encompasses all of these meanings. Gratitude is a thankful appreciation for what an individual receives, whether tangible or intangible. With gratitude, people acknowledge the goodness in their lives. In the process, people usually recognise that the source of that goodness lies at least partially outside themselves. As a result, gratitude also helps people connect to something larger than themselves as individuals – whether to other people, nature, or a higher power.

In positive psychology research, gratitude is strongly and consistently associated with greater happiness. Gratitude helps people feel more positive emotions, relish good experiences, improve their health, deal with adversity, and build strong relationships.

The Law of Attraction is a principle built on the supposition that we create our own reality. We attract those things that we 'put out'. What does this mean? Well, the simplest way of stating this principle is that like attracts like. If you are a happy, outgoing, and appreciative individual, with the frame of mind that you have all you need – then you will attract happiness, friends, blessings, and wealth.

Manifesting abundance begins with the right frame of mind. For this, you need to understand a principle called Stillness. The Stillness Effect is centred around mindful meditation, and how it can help you to overcome your own inner limitations and achieve abundance. When you regularly focus on quietening your mind, you teach yourself how to express gratitude, feel pure happiness, and adopt the right attitude to attract the things you want. It's really quite simple. Take some time to find out more about Stillness today.

Gratefulness is Uplifting

To be grateful is such an uplifting and grounding state of mind. It allows us to live in full appreciation of being alive, and being truly happy with what we have, however little that may be. This does not mean stopping ourselves trying to do better, or not allowing self-growth. We must always strive to be the best we can be, but be glad to have everything we do have.

Living your life with gratitude means choosing to focus your time and attention on what you appreciate. The goal is not to block out difficulties, but to approach those difficulties from a different perspective. Appreciation softens us. It soothes our turbulent minds by connecting us with the wonderfully ordinary things, great and small, that we might otherwise take for granted.

When our minds are calm and relaxed, it allows us to look at challenges with a more constructive and enabling view.

Gratitude can help us see that not everything is terrible – not all the time, anyway. Practising gratitude can keep our hearts open to the tenderness in our daily experiences. There are so many things to be grateful for. Just to wake up in the morning alive is something to be grateful for – daily over 150,000 people do not wake up the next day.

Offering our appreciation to one another is a powerful way to strengthen and even repair emotional bonds.

Practice gratitude daily. Indeed, many studies over the past decade have found that people who consciously count their blessings tend to be happier and less depressed.

Here are some simple gratitude tips:

1. **Say "thank you!"** Who doesn't want to be appreciated for their efforts? Saying thanks can be a gift, and one that feels pretty good, too!
2. **Remember what you appreciate most.** When you're feeling low, take a moment and write down some things that spark gratitude in you, like:
   - The pleasure of the spring sun.
   - A stirring piece of music or art.
   - A delicious or nutritious meal.

- A child's laughter, a stranger's sweet smile, a shared moment of joy.
3. **Pay attention to your emotions.** Describe in as much detail as possible how your body feels when you express gratitude. Which emotions accompany these bubbly feelings? What kind of thoughts do you notice? When you begin to turn more frequently towards the things you appreciate, the world increasingly opens to reveal that there is always some small thing for which you can be grateful.

"If you are not devoted you will not do anything significant in your life"

Philanthropy

Wikipedia definition – Philanthropy means the love of humanity. A conventional modern definition is "private initiatives, for the public good, focusing on quality of life", which combines an original humanistic tradition with a social scientific aspect developed in the 20th century.

What Qualifies Someone to be a Philanthropist?

A philanthropist is a person who donates time, money, experience, skills or talent to help create a better world. Anyone can be a philanthropist, regardless of status or net worth.

What is the Role of Philanthropy?

The purpose of philanthropy is to improve the well-being of humankind by preventing and solving social problems.

Philanthropy is not the same as charity. What is the difference between charity and philanthropy?

Charity focuses on eliminating the suffering caused by social problems, while philanthropy focuses on eliminating social problems. The difference between the proverbial gift of a fish to a hungry person versus teaching them how to fish.

Who Started Philanthropy?

In 1911 and 1913, both the Carnegie Corporation of New York (started by Andrew Carnegie with a donation of $125 million) and the Rockefeller Foundation (started by John D. Rockefeller with a donation of $35 million) are founded, mainstreaming the modern private foundation.

Corporate Philanthropy

Corporate philanthropy is a general term for the actions that businesses take to improve their communities and society in general. Corporate philanthropy can include donations of money or of time and labour at community centres or for improvement projects, or for fundraising for a cause.

While philanthropy costs the company, it also provides benefits for the company, community and employees. Understanding the significance of corporate philanthropy helps your company justify the expense to upper management and investors.

The 13 Most Philanthropic Companies in the World[20]

13. Coca-Cola
Total cash donation in 2015: $117.3 million (£87.5 million)

12. Merck
Total cash donation in 2015: $132.5 million (£98.8 million)

11. Citigroup
Total cash donation in 2015: $142.8 million (£106.5 million)

10. Alphabet
Total cash donation in 2015: $167.8 million (£125.1 million)

9. Bank of America
Total cash donation in 2015: $168.5 million (£125.7 million)

8. Microsoft
Total cash donation in 2017: $169 million (£126 million)

7. Chevron
Total cash donation in 2015: $168.5 million (£125.7 million)

6. JPMorgan Chase
Total cash donation in 2017: $250 million (£186.5 million)

5. ExxonMobil
Total cash donation in 2015: $168.5 million (£125.7 million)

4. Goldman Sachs
Total cash donation in 2015: $168.5 million (£125.7 million)

3. Wells Fargo
Total cash donation in 2017: $286.5 million (£213.7 million)

2. Walmart
Total cash donation in 2015: $301 million (£224.5 million)

1. Gilead Sciences
Total cash donation in 2015: $446.7 million (£333.2 million)

Who Are Some Famous Philanthropists?

Top 10[21]

1 Bill Gates
Lifetime donations: $27 billion
Net worth: $84.2 billion
Generosity Index: 32%

2 Warren Buffett
Lifetime donations: $21.5 billion
Net worth: $61 billion
Generosity Index: 35%

3 George Soros
Lifetime donations: $8 billion
Net worth: $24.4 billion
Generosity Index: 33%

4 Azim Premji
Lifetime donations: $7.5 billion
Net worth: $15.9 billion
Generosity Index: 50%

5 Charles Francis Feeney
Lifetime donations: $6.3 billion
Net worth: $1.5 million
Generosity Index: 420,000%
Known as the "James Bond of philanthropy", retail magnate Chuck Feeney is on a mission to give away his entire fortune – and his current net worth is down to $1.5 million.

6 Sulaiman bin Abdul Aziz Al Rajhi
Lifetime donations: $5.7 billion
Net worth: $590 million
Generosity Index: 966%
Back in 1957, Sulaiman bin Abdul Aziz Al Rajhi co-founded Al Rajhi Bank with his three brothers. It grew into one of the world's largest Islamic banks and earned Al Rajhi a 10-digit net worth.

7 Gordon Moore
Lifetime donations: $5 billion
Net worth: $6.5 billion
Generosity Index: 77%

8 Carlos Slim Helú
Lifetime donations: $4 billion
Net worth: $27.3 billion
Generosity Index: 15%

9 Eli Broad
Lifetime donations: $3.3 billion
Net worth: $7.3 billion
Generosity Index: 45%
Through the Broad Foundation, KB Home co-founder and former SunAmerica CEO Eli Broad invests in public education, science, and the arts.

10 George Kaiser
Lifetime donations: $3.3 billion
Net worth: $9.3 billion
Generosity Index: 35%
George Kaiser, chairman of BOK Financial Corporation, also founded the George Kaiser Family Foundation, which gives to educational, health, religious, social, and community development-related causes, including the Tulsa Community College Foundation, Oklahoma City Educare, National Energy Policy Institute, the Tulsa Community Foundation and the University of Tulsa.

Quotes from famous Philanthropists

"If you're in the luckiest 1% of humanity you owe it to the rest of humanity to think about the other 99%"

– Warren Buffett

"You want to be the pebble in the pond that creates the ripple for change"

– Tim Cook, Apple CEO

"Wealth is not to feed our egos, but to feed the hungry and to help people help themselves"

– Andrew Carnegie

"You look at things you enjoy in your life, but much more important is what you can do to make the world a better place"

– Paul Allen

"My goal in pledging 99% of my assets to philanthropy is to help others with roots – food, warmth, shelter, healthcare, education – so they too can have wings"

– Judy Faulkner

Further Quotes of Wisdom

"I am of the opinion that my life belongs to the community. And as long as I live, it is my privilege to do for it whatever I can. I want to be thoroughly used up when I die, for the harder I work, the more I live. Life is no brief candle to me; it is a sort of splendid torch, which I have got hold of for a short moment, and I want to make it burn as brightly as possible before handing it on to the future generations"

– George Bernard Shaw

"To laugh often and to love much; to win the respect of intelligent persons and the affection of children; to earn the approbation of honest critics and to endure the betrayal of false friends; to appreciate beauty; to find the best in others; to give of oneself; to leave the world a bit better, whether by a healthy child, a garden patch, or a redeemed social condition; to have played and laughed with enthusiasm and sung with exultation; to know that even one life has breathed easier because you have lived – this is to have succeeded"

– Ralph Waldo Emerson

"Every man must decide whether he will walk in the light of creative altruism or in the darkness of destructive selfishness"

– Martin Luther King Jr

"Philanthropy is commendable, but it must not cause the philanthropist to overlook the circumstances of economic injustice which make philanthropy necessary"

– Martin Luther King Jr

"One must be poor to know the luxury of giving"

– George Eliot

"It is one of the most beautiful compensations of this life that no man can sincerely try to help another without helping himself. ... Serve and thou shall be served"

– Ralph Waldo Emerson

"One must know not just how to accept a gift, but with what grace to share it"

– Maya Angelou

"To give away money is an easy matter and in any man's power. But to decide to whom to give it and how large and when, and for what purpose and how, is neither in every man's power nor an easy matter"

– Aristotle

"The desire of power in excess caused the angels to fall; the desire of knowledge in excess caused man to fall: but in charity there is no excess; neither can angel nor man come in danger by it"

– Francis Bacon

"Every dollar makes a difference. And that's true whether it's Warren Buffet's remarkable $31 billion pledge to the Gates Foundation or my late father's $25 cheque to the NAACP"

– Michael Bloomberg

"The test of a civilisation is in the way that it cares for its helpless members"

– Pearl S. Buck

"Real generosity towards the future lies in giving all to the present"

– Albert Camus

"No one is useless in this world who lightens the burdens of another"

– Charles Dickens

"It is every man's obligation to put back into the world at least the equivalent of what he takes out of it"

– Albert Einstein

"A man wrapped up in himself makes a very small bundle"

– Benjamin Franklin

"Each time a man stands up for an ideal, or acts to improve the lot of others, or strikes out against injustice, he sends forth a tiny ripple of hope, and crossing each other from a million different centres of energy and daring, those ripples build a current that can sweep down the mightiest walls of oppression and resistance

– Robert Kennedy

"To pity distress is but human; to relieve it is Godlike"

– Horace Mann

"Charity is injurious unless it helps the recipient to become independent of it"

– John D. Rockefeller

"If you want to lift yourself up, lift up someone else"

– Booker T. Washington

"We can all make a difference in the lives of others in need, because it is the simplest of gestures that make the most significant of differences"

– Miya Yamanouchi

"Nothing brings me more happiness than trying to help the most vulnerable people in society. It is a goal and an essential part of my life – a kind of destiny. Whoever is in distress can call on me. I will come running wherever they are"

– Princess Diana

"Generosity is the flower of justice"

– Nathaniel Hawthorne

"Do your little bit of good where you are; it's those little bits of good put together that overwhelm the world"

– Desmond Tutu

Famous Charity Workers

A list of famous charity workers. People who helped others to lead better lives.

Mother Teresa (1910-1997) – Mother Teresa founded the Missionaries of Charity and dedicated her life to serving the poor in India and around the world.

"Let us not be satisfied with just giving money. Money is not enough, money can be got, but they need your hearts to love them. So, spread your love everywhere you go"

– **Mother Teresa**

Clara Barton (1821-1912) – A nurse in the American Civil War, Clara Barton helped improve treatment of wounded soldiers. After working with the international Red Cross in Europe, she returned to the US, where she set up the American Red Cross.

William Booth (1829-1912) – Founder of the Salvation Army. Booth dedicated his life to offering charitable support to the poor in London. A fervent evangelical Christian, he was committed to providing material aid and spiritual salvation.

Bill Wilson (1896-1971) – Co-founder of Alcoholics Anonymous, an international organisation with over two million members seeking to help individuals escape from alcoholism. Wilson found a cure for his own alcoholism and set up self-help groups to enable others to do the same. He did not seek to raise money, but give people the support to give up alcohol.

Cecil Jackson-Cole (1901-1979) – Co-founder of Oxfam. Jackson-Cole revolutionised the charitable sector, launching professional management and charity shops which sold tradecraft from developing countries. Jackson-Cole was also instrumental in founding Help the Aged/Age Concern. In 1972, he also started a new charitable initiative, ActionAid, which matched sponsors in developed countries with poor children in developing economies.

Abbé Pierre (1912-2007) – French humanitarian who founded the charity Emmaus movement to help refugees and the homeless. Pierre wanted to not just give material help, but the resources for people to help themselves. A saying of the Emmaus movement is: "Giving people a bed and a reason to get out of it".

Chad Varah (1911-2007) – British vicar who founded the Samaritans, an organisation offering an opportunity for the suicidal to speak in confidence. Varah founded the organisation in 1953 after taking calls in his church. He was also committed to supporting sex education.

Eva Peron (1919-1952) – The Eva Peron Foundation raised millions to fund orphanages, hospitals and schools. The Foundation aimed to 'contribute or collaborate by any possible means to the creation of works tending to satisfy the basic needs for better life of the less privileged classes.'

Audrey Hepburn (1929-1993) – Audrey Hepburn supported UNICEF from the 1950s. In the latter part of her life, she retired from acting to devote more time to UNICEF projects in Africa and other countries.

"The 'Third World' is a term I don't like very much because we're all one world. I want people to know that the largest part of humanity is suffering"

– **Audrey Hepburn**

Princess Diana (1961-1997) – Princess Diana was associated with many hundreds of charities. She paid particular attention to charities involved with AIDS, landmines, prisoners' families and palliative care.

"I knew what my job was; it was to go out and meet the people and love them"

– **Princess Diana**

Bono (*b* 1960) – Bono is involved in various charities, including DATA (Debt, AIDS, Trade, Africa), established in 2002 with Bobby Shriver. DATA aims to eradicate poverty and HIV/AIDS in Africa. Also involved in Drop the Debt campaign.

Joan Baez (*b* 1941) – Joan Baez is a singer-songwriter whose career spanned six decades. In the 1970s she played a key role in founding the US version of Amnesty International. Later, she formed her own human rights organisation, Humanitas International.

Bob Geldof (*b* 1951) – Bob Geldof was moved by African famine in 1984. He released the hit single "Do They Know It's Christmas" and organised 'Live Aid'. He has been involved in various charities ever since.

Oprah Winfrey (*b* 1954) – Oprah has donated millions of her own fortune for charities such as Angel Network and a charity helping young girls gain an education in South Africa.

Angelina Jolie (*b* 1975) – Jolie has worked with the United Nations High Commissioner for Refugees (UNHCR). She also founded charities such as Maddox Jolie-Pitt Foundation community development and environmental conservation in Cambodia.

Jane Goodall (*b* 1934) – Jane Goodall is a noted humanitarian, environmentalist, and has spent many years observing the behaviour of chimpanzees in their native habitat.

"Chimpanzees have given me so much. The long hours spent with them in the forest have enriched my life beyond measure. What I have learned from them has shaped my understanding of human behaviour, of our place in nature"

– **Jane Goodall**

Desmond Tutu (*b* 1931) – Desmond Mpilo Tutu was born in Klerksdorp, Transvaal, South Africa, on 7th October 1931. As a vocal and committed opponent of apartheid in South Africa, Tutu was awarded the Nobel Peace Prize in 1984. In the transition to democracy, Tutu was an influential figure in promoting the concept of forgiveness and reconciliation. Tutu has been recognised as the 'moral conscience of South Africa' and frequently speaks up on issues of justice and peace.

Florence Nightingale (1820-1910) – Volunteered to nurse soldiers during the Crimean War. Nightingale's analysis of mortality rates helped to improve hospital practices. She also helped improve the standard and prestige of the nursing profession. She is considered to be the founder of modern nursing.

Global Growth & Giving

WORLD'S TOP 10 MOST GENEROUS COUNTRIES

The CAF World Giving Index, the leading comparative study of global generosity, records the number of people who helped a stranger in the past month, volunteered their time (21.1%, up from 20.8% last year) or gave money to a good cause (29.1%, down slightly from 29.6% last year). This year more than 150,000 people in 146 countries were surveyed as part of the Gallup World Poll. As a result, the Index highlights statistically significant global shifts in behaviour, even when changes may appear to be small.

- This year's Index shows high levels of generosity in Haiti, with the country featuring in the top 20 for the first time.
- Singapore also features in the top 20 for the first time this year, having ranked as low as 64th place just five years ago. There have been increases in volunteering and helping a stranger, which may be as a result of a number of schemes to increase volunteering in the country over recent years.
- Libya was the most generous in terms of helping a stranger, where 83% of people reported having done so.

The Index, now in its ninth year, shows high levels of generosity in some countries experiencing civil war, conflict and unrest, showing how the human urge to help others comes through even in some of the most troubled nations on Earth.

In many countries, men remain more likely than women to have volunteered time (22.6% compared with 19.5%), but the slight global increase in volunteering time has been driven more by women, who increased their participation rate by 0.5 percentage points year on year. There is, however,

Table 1. Top 20 countries in the CAF World Giving Index with score and participation in giving behaviours.

	CAF World Giving Index ranking	CAF World Giving Index score (%)	Helping a stranger (%)	Donating money (%)	Volunteering time (%)
Indonesia	1	59%	46%	78%	53%
Australia	2	59%	65%	71%	40%
New Zealand	3	58%	66%	68%	40%
United States of America	4	58%	72%	61%	39%
Ireland	5	56%	64%	64%	40%
United Kingdom	6	55%	63%	68%	33%
Singapore	7	54%	67%	58%	39%
Kenya	8	54%	72%	46%	45%
Myanmar	9	54%	40%	88%	34%
Bahrain	10	53%	74%	53%	33%
Netherlands	11	51%	52%	66%	37%
United Arab Emirates	12	51%	68%	62%	23%
Norway	13	50%	54%	65%	32%
Haiti	14	49%	62%	54%	31%
Canada	15	49%	57%	56%	33%
Nigeria	16	48%	71%	36%	37%
Iceland	17	48%	50%	65%	27%
Malta	18	47%	53%	64%	25%
Liberia	19	47%	80%	14%	47%
Sierra Leone	20	47%	80%	23%	37%

little difference between men and women when it comes to donating money.

Sir John Low, Chief Executive of the Charities Aid Foundation, an international charity which helps people and companies give worldwide, said:

"It is forever humbling to see how people across the world continue to be moved to help others, giving their time, donating money and helping strangers. It is a basic human instinct to lend a helping hand, and it is always amazing to see how people in countries which have suffered conflict and natural disasters are stirred to help those in need. It is good news that this year's CAF World Giving Index shows a continued increase in giving across Africa. It is also encouraging that last year's decline in Western countries seems to have been reversed. But we should be concerned that for the second year running there has been a decline in the proportion of people donating money to good causes. It is a reminder to all of us in civil society that we should never take giving for granted."

Methodology

The World Giving Index is primarily based on data from Gallup's World Poll, which is an on-going research project carried out in more than 146 countries in 2017 that together represent around 95% of the world's population (around 5.2 billion people). The survey asks questions on many different aspects of life today, including giving behaviour.

The World's Most Generous Countries

Myanmar
Myanmar has consistently claimed the title for the most generous country in the world for the last four years. Although it is a lower middle-income country with little resources to compete with the superpowers, it confounded the traditional assumption that ties generosity with wealth. A whopping 91% of the population reported that they had donated money to charity in 2016. Myanmar's generosity is linked to the popularity of Buddhism in the country. It is common in the country for one to give food, money, and other material support to the monks.

Indonesia and Malta
Coming distant second is Indonesia with 79% of the population giving towards charity and in third place are the Maltese with 73% of the population. Indonesia ranked second for the second consecutive year in terms of money donated was the highest ranked among the G20's largest economy. Indonesia's high ranking may have been as a result of the survey being conducted in the August, the month of Ramadan, when most people are expected to give to charity. Charity donation in Malta was boosted by the tax deductions on donations to cultural sectors.

Iceland, Thailand, and New Zealand
Between 65 and 68% of the populations of Iceland,

Thailand, and New Zealand gave to charity in 2016. Iceland, through non-profit organisations, has set up several charitable organisations such as Iceland Food Charitable Foundation that receive the donation and distribute to the people in need, both locally and abroad. Thailand, one of the emerging markets, made a comeback to the top ten and has been focusing on children's health and education as major areas of support among other areas with 68% of the population donating towards the needy.

Other Top Generous Countries

Netherlands, **United Kingdom**, **Australia**, and **Canada** complete the list of top ten most generous countries with at least 60% of their population donating money to charity. Canada returned to the top ten in 2016 after missing out in the previous year. However, it recorded the worst ever participation rate in 2016 at 61%.

Top Generous Countries by Number of People

Although Myanmar is the most generous country by the proportion of the population, India had the highest number of people giving to charity. 265 million people in India donated, compared to 34 million people in Myanmar. In fact, Myanmar would rank tenth if the number of people was considered. Indonesia would retain its position, with 146 million people donating. About 144 million people in the US donated in monetary form, while 91 million Chinese also donated their money to charity.

The 10 Most Generous Countries

Rank	Country	Population Donating to Charity
1	Myanmar	91%
2	Indonesia	79%
3	Malta	73%
4	Iceland	68%
5	Thailand	68%
6	New Zealand	65%
7	Netherlands	64%
8	United Kingdom	64%
9	Australia	63%
10	Canada	61%

Obsession with Economic Growth

At the University of Kansas in March 1968, a few months before he was shot, the then-presidential candidate Robert Kennedy said – *"GDP measures neither our wit nor our courage, neither our wisdom nor our learning, neither our compassion nor our devotion to our country; it measures everything in short, except that which makes life worthwhile."*

Fifty years on and we are still obsessed with this flawed metric as the key indicator of economic success. We still think "bigger is better", that higher GDP is the solution to our problems.

Over the decades since his speech, deepening inequality across the globe has worsened. In China, while growth has taken hundreds of millions out of poverty, growing inequity – including income inequality levels among the worst in the world – is tolerated because GDP growth remains strong.

Likewise, in the US, the super-rich have accumulated obscene levels of wealth without any redistribution to lower-paid and less-skilled workers who haven't benefited from globalisation.

GDP, which measures the dollar value of goods and services produced by a nation, measures none of the practical outcomes such as the well-being of communities. Nor does GDP adjust for how the benefits are distributed. Two very different economies, one with obscene levels of inequality and another with more equitable wealth distribution, could have the same GDP per capita. Also, no adjustment for leisure time is made; for example, imagine a country where the average number of hours worked per day is 5 and a country where the average is 10 – where would you prefer to live?

GDP also does not account for unpaid caring and domestic work, which props up the economy. Nor does it account for the informal or black-market activity that can represent a significant part of overall economic activity in some less-developed economies.

It also pays no attention to environmental costs. Two economies can have the same GDP per capita, but one has massive pollution of soil, air and water and the other doesn't, and their citizens' well-being will be different. GDP per capita will not capture that difference.

Joseph Stiglitz, as Nobel Prize in Economics laureate, and MIT's Erik Brynjolfsson noted in 2016, *"GDP is a poor way of assessing the health of our economies, and we urgently need to find a new measure."*

An alternative measure does exist. Since the 1970s, the tiny Himalayan kingdom of Bhutan has rejected GDP as the sole way to measure progress. Instead, it has implemented a Gross National Happiness Index; the aim is to find a way to govern and live which looks beyond narrow economic metrics. The indicators on which it gathers data range from psychological well-being, culture and education to ecology and community vitality.

United Nations Development Programme, through its Human Development Index, measures those factors that make a good life beyond just income. It takes into account a country's life expectancy at birth, the adult literacy rate, and the standard of living.

The World Happiness Report, produced by the UN Sustainable Development Solutions Network, offers an annual index ranking countries on factors including social support, healthy life expectancy, freedom, trust and generosity, in addition to income. And the Organisation for Economic Co-operation and Development produces a Better Life Index, which allows people to compare well-being across countries based on factors the organisation deems essential to quality of life, including housing, community, health and environment.

We need to fundamentally change the way we think about the economy. The dominant economic thinking of the past century is characterised as the pursuit of narrow self-interests – whether of a person, an organisation or a country. The challenges we face, however, require an awareness that goes far beyond the self, to one that considers the whole economic system.

Questioning the Growth Model

Two of the world's biggest fund management bosses have called for a rethink of capitalism and its obsession with constant economic growth, in an appeal for business and governments to deal more decisively with the challenges of climate change.

Anne Richards, chief executive of Fidelity International, said the world must end "our obsession with ever-increasing GDP" and the "primacy of shareholders" to foster the kind of long-term thinking that would help protect the environment.

Andreas Utermann, CEO of Allianz Global Investors, said the world's growth mania – "nominal GDP growth, supported by population growth, and profit growth" – was clearly unsustainable, and suggested that capitalism in its current form is "borrowing from the future while destroying the environment".

And raising this to another level, in the *New York Review of Books*, David Graeber asks if current economics as a discipline is even able to cope with the challenge of climate reality. Economic theory as it exists increasingly resembles a shed full of broken tools. This is not to say there are no useful insights here, but fundamentally the existing discipline is designed to solve another century's problems. The problem of how to determine the optimal distribution of work and resources to create high levels of economic growth is simply not the same problem we are now facing: i.e., how to deal with increasing technological productivity, decreasing real demand for labour, and the effective management of care work, without also destroying the Earth. Presumably, some kind of shock would be required. What might it take? Another 2008-style collapse? Some radical political shift in a major world government? A global youth rebellion?

Vision for Leadership in Business

The ethical leader understands that positive relationships are the gold standard for all organisational effort. Good quality relationships built on respect and trust – not necessarily agreement. The ethical leader understands that these kinds of relationships germinate and grow in the deep rich soil of fundamental principles: trust, respect, integrity, honesty, fairness, equity, justice and compassion. Early last century, the German philosopher and theologian, Martin Buber, described these successful relationships as "I-Thou" relationships, in which people recognise the intrinsic worth and value of others and treat each other with sincerity and respect.[23] In the language of the 18th century German philosopher, Immanuel Kant, this is the principle of always treating the other person as an end and never merely as a means to serve your own personal interests.[24]

The ethical leader moves and acts in a world of I-Thou relationships, where in any situation, to the fullest extent possible in the circumstances, the intent is to honour and respect the worth of the other person.

Principles of Ethical Work Practices

- Don't separate ethics from day-to-day business: Business people must make it clear to their employees that ethics is "the way we operate" and not a training programme or reference manual. Every activity, whether it is a training programme, a client meeting or an important top management strategy session, should include conversations about ethics.

- Don't think about ethics as just following laws and regulations: Business people need to act and show consumers and other stakeholders that they are actively engaged with ethical issues that matter. Recognise how ethics influences consumers' reasons to buy from you and demonstrate a commitment to go beyond mere compliance with laws and regulations.
- Don't exempt anyone from meeting ethical expectations: Allow no excuses. Make sure that no one is exempted from meeting the ethical standards that are adopted. Maintain the status of ethics as a total, absolute, "must do" in the organisation.
- Celebrate positive ethical moments: Be a proactive ethical business person, championing high ethical conduct and emphasising prevention.
- Talk about ethics as an on-going learning journey. We must accept that every business decision and action we take has a consequence; the consequence must not just be profit with the motto that more is better. We need to consider how it will affect our fellow humans, be they employees, tenants, neighbours, business partners and all – this outlook will enable us to move in the right direction, leading to a fairer and more just society.

"Consume what you can digest — consumerism pushes us to have what you cannot digest."

Social Capitalism

Social Capitalism can be defined as a socially minded form of capitalism, where the goal is making social improvements, rather than focusing on accumulating of capital in the classic capitalist sense. It is a utilitarian form of capitalism with a social purpose. You could think of this as egalitarian economic practices that aim to ameliorate the social problems caused by capitalism, primarily inequity.

Social capitalism is related or associated with the Third Way,[25] the humanisation of capitalism, democratic capitalism, and social democracy. This would describe a practical midway point between "late-form capitalism" and "socialism".

Social capitalism is not a top-down regulation of capitalism for the social good. It is a deliberate choice made by individuals to promote equality, fairness, and justice for all. It is a choice to improve societal and environmental outcomes for the betterment of all, including future generations. It is a value system, not an economic or political system.

What Does Social Capitalism Look Like?

It is not socialism, and it is not capitalism. It is not charity, nor is it philanthropy. It is about directing capital towards the common benefit via markets as individuals and collectives.

It is about solving social issues and making a profit, and has an ideology of liberty, equality, and justice.

Liberty because all action is elective, equality because anyone can be a social capitalist and no group is excluded from its benefits, justice because it is moral and ethical to care for the public good, and utilitarian because its ends are ethically-based happiness for the many.

Social capitalism is about:
- Non-profit companies working to solve a social or environmental issue, or redirecting profit back to the public good.
- For-profit companies that choose improved social and/or environmental outcomes even when it doesn't maximise profit. And for-profit companies that redirect some profit back to the public good.
- Investment in companies that are socially and/or environmentally responsible, or at least those that do not create social or environmental problems or exploit these for profit.
- Working for or with companies that are socially and environmentally ethical and care for the public good.

- Actively seeking out and purchasing products from companies that are socially and environmentally ethical and care for the public good, while boycotting companies that do not.
- Actively talking about and sharing information about ethical companies to encourage others to engage with or buy from them.
- Actively sharing information about unethical companies to discourage others from engaging with them.
- Valuing people for more than their labour or profit they can make a company. It is about creating a positive empowering culture that allows people to be happy and reach their potential.
- Replacing short-term goals that result in exploitation with long-term goals that support investment, growth, and sustainable prosperity.

With this in mind, the social market economy is a social and economic system combining free market capitalism which supports private enterprise, alongside social policies which establish both fair competition within the market and a welfare state. It is sometimes classified as a co-ordinated market economy.

Social capital can also provide access to human capital, in the form of skills, expertise, knowledge, or information.

Social capital is a positive product of human interaction. The term social capital is also sometimes used to describe the personal relationships within a company that help build trust and respect among employees, leading to enhanced company performance.

Without us noticing, we are entering the post-capitalist era. At the heart of further change to come is information technology, new ways of working and the sharing economy.

The process technology has created a new route out, which the remnants of the old left – and all other forces influenced by it – have either to embrace or die. Capitalism, it turns out, will not be abolished by force. It will be abolished by creating something more dynamic that exists, at first, almost unseen within the old system, but which will break through, reshaping the economy around new values and behaviours. This is post-capitalism. Capitalism's replacement by post-capitalism will be accelerated by external shocks and shaped by the emergence of a new kind of human being.

Post-capitalism is possible because of three major changes that information technology has brought about in the past 25 years.

First, it has reduced the need for work, blurred the edges between work and free time and loosened the relationship between work and wages; this is the coming wave of automation, which will hugely diminish the amount of work needed.

Second, information is corroding the market's ability to form prices correctly.

This is because the markets are based on scarcity while information is abundant.

Third, we're seeing the spontaneous rise of collaborative production: goods, services and organisations are appearing that no longer respond to the dictates of the market and the managerial hierarchy. The biggest information product in the world – Wikipedia – is made by volunteers for free, abolishing the encyclopaedia business and depriving the advertising industry of an estimated $3bn a year in revenue.

The 2008 crash wiped 13% off global production and 20% off global trade. Global growth became negative – on a scale where anything below +3% is counted as a recession. It produced, in the West, a depression phase longer than in 1929-33.[26]

Meanwhile, in the absence of any alternative model, the conditions for another crisis are being assembled. Real wages have fallen or remained stagnant in Japan, the southern Eurozone, the US and UK. The shadow banking system has been reassembled, and is now bigger than it was in 2008.

New rules demanding banks hold more reserves have been watered down or delayed. Meanwhile, flushed with free money, the 1% has got richer.

Circular Economy to Save the World

Each year, the fashion industry alone loses $500bn due to clothing becoming waste.[27] In the plastics sector, 95 percent of packaging material value is lost to the economy after a first-use cycle, equating to $80-120bn each year.[28]

Transforming our linear economy into a circular economy offers a huge opportunity to recapture this value by designing out waste and pollution, keeping products and materials in use, and regenerating natural systems. If we acknowledge that waste and pollution are the results of issues overlooked during product design, it follows that we can choose to view waste and pollution as a design flaw instead of an inevitable outcome. We can then innovate our way towards its elimination.

Take a drinks bottle, for example. Instead of being designed to be thrown away, it can be designed so that it can be sent back to the bottler, to be washed and refilled. The bottle can be designed to be more durable, so it lasts longer and can be reused many times. When it reaches the end of its usable life, the materials that make up the bottle can then be recovered and remanufactured into a new one. For fast-moving consumer goods, like bottled drinks, there is an estimated material cost saving potential of up to $700bn globally in a circular economy.[29]

To keep more complex products and materials in use for longer, we can also rethink product ownership. Take a car, for example. The average European car is parked 92% of the time, meaning it is significantly under-utilised. For most people, the important thing is having access to transport, not owning the materials that can make up the car. Car manufacturers can sell mobility as a service rather than selling cars. By moving to a shared transport model, car utilisation can be increased, and because the vehicles are still owned by the manufacturer, can be designed to last as long as possible and be repaired and remanufactured.

We can also design out waste and pollution in our biological systems, starting by rethinking how we produce and consume food. Imagine a food system where you can not only enjoy a delicious and nutritious meal, but where all of the ingredients also help to tackle climate change and biodiversity loss. A system that regenerates nature instead of degrading it, and enables food to be sourced locally when appropriate, where we make the most of our food.

By 2050, 80 per cent of food is expected to be consumed in cities. Cities are also hubs for businesses whose innovation capabilities can drive the transformation of the food system. Food product developers within brands and chefs in restaurants can design product menus that support environmental regeneration and waste elimination. Through sourcing, they can support regenerative farming practices that move us away from a system that impacts the health of our ecosystems to one that rebuilds them.

Regenerative farming is most associated with the creation of healthy soil, but it also incorporates practices such as agroforestry – trees and shrubs grown near crops to improve biodiversity and limit land erosion – and new seafood production methods that benefit marine ecosystems. It also has the potential to reduce annual greenhouse gas emissions by the equivalent of permanently taking nearly one billion cars off the road.

To unlock the economic, societal, and environmental benefits of such a transition in our European food system, an investment of €70bn is expected to be needed. While this is significant, globally, actions taken by cities alone towards a circular economy for food could generate annual economic, environmental and health benefits worth $2.7 trillion by 2050.

The potential for a return on investment in a circular economy across systems has encouraged pioneering financial institutions to step forward to accelerate change. Italian banking group Intesa Sanpaolo has committed to helping redefine business strategies and to provide financial support for investments, addressing the redesign of the industrial system. The EU has allocated €650m for circular economy research and innovation under Horizon 2020, and €5.5bn under Structural and Investment Funds for waste management. Most recently, investment management company, BlackRock, launched its first circular economy fund with the Ellen MacArthur Foundation, driving investments in businesses already contributing to, or benefiting from, the transition to a circular economy. With funds being targeted towards the growth of a circular economy, it is time for us all to consider the role we can play in designing out waste and pollution, keeping materials and products in use, and regenerating natural systems. We have a unique opportunity to secure a better future for businesses, society and the environment, moving away from our reliance on finite resources. I believe we can succeed in tackling the challenges that face us by seizing the opportunity to redesign our global economy and by acting now.

Benefits of Organisational Giving

Organisations have a strong interest in fostering a giving behaviour. A willingness to help others achieve their goals lies at the heart of effective collaboration, innovation, quality improvement, and service excellence. In workplaces where such behaviour becomes the norm, the benefits multiply quickly. Consider a landmark meta-analysis led by Nathan Podsakoff, of the University of Arizona.[30] His team examined 38 studies of organisational behaviour, representing more than 3,500 business units and many different industries, and found that the link between employee giving and desirable business outcomes was surprisingly robust. Higher rates of giving were predictive of higher unit profitability, productivity, efficiency, and customer satisfaction, along with lower costs and turnover rates. When employees act like givers, they facilitate efficient problem-solving and co-ordination and build cohesive, supportive cultures that appeal to customers, suppliers, and top talent alike.

Further Benefits

- Successful givers produced 50% more annual revenue, on average, than colleagues who focused less on helping others. In both cases, generosity appeared to sink some

employees to the bottom while propelling others to the top.
- One of the critical distinctions between self-sacrificing givers and successful ones is the willingness to seek help from others.
- The more an employee becomes known for offering specific kinds of help, the less likely people are to pile on miscellaneous requests.

Giving Something Back: raising the profile of your business through good works

For many people who are working in small businesses, the idea of 'giving back' or working with 'corporate social responsibility', as large businesses call it, is something that comes perfectly naturally. Small businesses tend to be more generous and more socially and culturally aware, simply because they are such an integral part of the community and the cultures that exist around themselves. Just by being a small business or an SME you are probably (hopefully) already making a positive contribution to both the environment and the community in your vicinity.

With big companies, you see them actually creating policies that perhaps, reduce waste and recycle more, or that allow their employees to take part in voluntary activities such as mentoring or working for a charity. Some particularly enlightened employers allow employees to take time off to do this.

The presence of millennials in the workforce is rapidly increasing; currently, they hold about 20 percent of all leadership roles, and that percentage is set to sharply increase in 2021. They're the most desirable commodity in the workplace, but can no longer be attracted by traditional benefit schemes. The age-old company car isn't going to cut it when trying to entice millennials to an organisation – they're looking for more than just money and copy-and-paste work perks. As the most diverse generation yet, they're pushing for the organisations that they work for to reflect that.

It's been well documented that millennials are attracted to purpose over profit – and studies have shown that inspired employees are almost three times more productive than dissatisfied ones.[31] Millennials want the businesses that they work for to do what they say they will and act responsibly. In fact, 52 percent of millennials said that they would consider leaving their current job for one that had more positive impact. Meanwhile, the average employee stays in their job for about five years, with millennials spending significantly less time in each role.

The Business Benefits of Giving

Millennials are looking for companies that have a social purpose that is authentic and inclusive of everyone within the organisation. While many companies offer their employees the option to volunteer during work hours, there has been plenty of research into the benefits of donating over volunteering. Essentially, it is far more effective and efficient to donate to charities and allow the experts in their field to use the funding to positively impact as many people as possible.

New research has revealed that the more SMEs give to charity, the better their business performs.

SMEs that give more than 0.5 percent turnover are 20 percent more likely to see an increase in profits, twice as likely to report benefits to company reputation, and almost 50 percent more likely to improve recruitment and staff retention. Overall, 68 per cent of businesses who give to charity reported a positive impact on profitability.[32]

SMEs can remain ahead of the curve and attract the best talent and boost their profits by thinking creatively about how best to demonstrate their commitment to social impact.

Giving to Your Employees

To recruit and harness the potential of employees is crucial to any business success; an organisation is the sum total of the quality and dynamism of its employees. Recruiting, engaging, and enthusing staff with commitment and a desire to give their best to promote the company they work for needs employees to feel more than salaried staff. This can be enabled through the creation of a group that is inter-giving, with a greater cause than just the bottom-line; this is particularly true in the current transformational capitalist world in which we find ourselves.

A term "Servant Leadership", first coined by Robert Greenleaf in 1970,[33] has been used widely since to describe a leader who is a giver. A leader who empathises and sees the potential of his employees and enables their growth within the organisation and within themselves. This type of leader is seen more of as a partner, therefore creating a feeling of camaraderie and cohesiveness within the organisation.

Research shows that companies that have incorporated employee inclusivity and participation within their work culture have done 8 times better in terms of return on investment as compared to the S&P 500 firms within a 10-year period.

Make Giving a Part of Your Life

Through acts of daily giving in your personal and professional life, tap into the unlimited nature and abundance you have within you. Create purpose and meaning in your professional and personal life.

Make giving part of who you are.

"Giving back is as good for you as it is for those you are helping, because giving gives you purpose. When you have a purpose-driven life, you're a happier person."

Giving can make you feel great, and if you give with a pure heart, you will be blessed financially. The important thing is to see the need for giving and to want to give. Helping others is not only good for them and a good thing to do, it also makes us happier and healthier, too. Giving also connects us to others, creating stronger communities and helping to build a happier society for everyone. And it's not all about money – we can also give our time, ideas and energy. For centuries, the greatest thinkers have suggested the same thing: Happiness is found in helping others.

Find Your Passion

Our passion should be the foundation for our giving. It is not *how much* we give, but *how much love* we put into giving. It's only natural that we will care about this and not so much about that, and that's OK. It should not be simply a matter of choosing the right thing, but also a matter of choosing what is right for us.

Give Your Time

The gift of time is often more valuable to the receiver and more satisfying for the giver than the gift of money. We don't all have the same amount of money, but we all do have time on our hands, and can give some of this time to help others – whether that means we devote our lifetimes to service, or just give a few hours each day or a few days a year.

Find Ways to Integrate Your Interests and Skills with the Needs of Others

"Selfless giving, in the absence of self-preservation instincts, easily becomes overwhelming," says Adam Grant, author of *Give & Take*.[34] It is important to be willing to give more than you receive, but still keeping your own interests in sight.

Be Proactive, Not Reactive

We have all felt the dread that comes from being cajoled into giving, such as when friends ask us to donate to their fundraisers. In these cases, we are more likely to give to avoid humiliation rather than out of generosity and concern. This type of giving doesn't lead to a warm-glow feeling; more likely it will lead to resentment. Instead, we should set aside time, think about our options, and find the best charity for our values.

Purpose, Meaning and Happiness

If we are feeling guilt-tripped into giving, chances are we will not be very committed over time to the cause. The key is to find the approach that fits us. When we do, then the more we give, the more we stand to gain in purpose, meaning and happiness.

Thank You

Thank you for giving me the opportunity and your time to share with you the meaning and importance of "Giving". I hope this short book has given you some inspiration to give and create abundance. To give is a beautiful experience; it is a wonderful powerful feeling to give regularly – this allows us to take the focus away from ourselves and self-centredness which ultimately only creates unhappiness. Give to yourself and to all around you as much and as often as you can. Once you experience the Power of Giving, it will positively transform your life.

"Do all the good you can. By all the means you can. In all the ways you can. In all the places you can. At all the times you can. To all the people you can. As long as ever you can"

— **John Wesley**

Supported Charitable Organisations

Hestia

Hestia began providing support to adults in crisis in 1970 after founder Jim Horne experienced street homelessness in London. He started a soup-run for men and women living on the streets and worked with local authorities to provide accommodation. Within the year, over 800 people were provided with a safe space to sleep at night.

Since then, Hestia has grown to support almost 11,000 adults and children in crisis across London every year. They provide support for those experiencing domestic abuse, modern slavery and mental health needs.

Hestia is one of the largest providers of domestic abuse refuges in London and the South-East, and is the main organisation supporting victims of modern slavery in the capital.

Hestia provides high-quality support for adults and children in crisis across London. Working in collaboration with local authorities and our partners, they strive to ensure that everyone within their care is equipped with the tools necessary for a life beyond a crisis. Their staff and volunteers build honest, respectful relationships with the service users to support and encourage them to lead their own recovery process.

Dar Lekbira Orphanage, Morocco

Dar Lekbira Orphanage has been established for several years in Kenitra, a city which is 30 minutes by train from the capital Rabat, North West Morocco. It houses and supports 120 orphaned children, teenagers and young adults. The orphanage houses and educates children from two years old to young adults. Abandoned by their family or driven away because of domestic violence, every child lives in the centre for a different reason.

Morocco's adoption laws are strict and children find themselves living in the orphanage for years.

In the majority of cases, orphans or abandoned children are left behind or marginalised in society.

There are approximately 65,000 orphans across Morocco.

REFERENCES

[1] BLOOM, Benjamin, "The Role of Gifts and Markers in the Development of Talent", *Exceptional Children*, vol 48, no 6, pp 510-522, April 1982.

[2] www.wikipedia.org/wiki/Risk_factors_for_suicide

[3] UK Office for National Statistics. www.ons.gov.uk/2018registrations

[4] For example, STEPHENS, Karen, "Parents Are Powerful Role Models for Children", *ParentingExchange.com*

[5] For example, WEINSTEIN, Netta, DE HAAN, Cody R., and RYAN, Richard M., "Attributing Autonomous Versus Injected Motivation to Helpers and the Recipient Experience", *Motivation and Emotion*, vol 34, no 4, pp 418-431.

[6] *Drug Overdose Deaths in the United States, 1999-2017*, Data Brief No 329, November 2018, The National Center for Health Statistics.

[7] For example, see SANTI, Jenny, *The Giving Way to Happiness*, Penguin, 2015.

[8] LUKS, Allan, "Doing Good: Helper's High", *Psychology Today*, vol 22, no 10, 1988.

[9] BENSON, Herbert, *The Relaxation Response*, William Morrow & Co, 1975.

[10] HARBAUGH, William T., MAYR, Ulrich, and BURGHART, Daniel R., "Neural Responses to Taxation and Voluntary Giving Reveal Motives for Charitable Donations", *Science*, vol 316, no 5331, pp 1622-1625, 15th June 2007.

[11] "5 Things That Happen When You Suppress Your Emotions", www.powerofpositivity.com/things-happen-suppress-emotions

[12] Quoted in NIVEN, David, *The 100 Simple Secrets of Successful People*, HarperOne, 2009.

[13] For example, see www.charitynavigator.org/index.cfm?bay=content.view&cpid=42: "Giving Statistics", where they state that "the majority of [the] giving came from individuals".

[14] For a wider discussion on "givers", "takers" and "matchers", see GRANT, Adam, *Give and Take: A Revolutionary Approach to Success*, Viking, 2013.

[15] CHATTERJEE, Arijit, and HAMBRICK, Donald C., "It's All About Me: Narcissistic Chief Executive Officers…", *Administrative Science Quarterly*, vol 52, no 3, pp 351-386, September 2007.

[16] See, for example, TELFORD, Olivia, *Mindfulness: The Remarkable Truth Behind Meditation and Being Present in Your Life*, independently published, 2019.

[17] See, for example, VESTERGAARD-POULSEN, Peter, VAN BEEK, Martin, SKEWES, Joshua, and BJARKAM, Carsten R., "Long-Term Meditation is Associated with Increased Gray Matter Density in the Brain Stem", *Neuroreport*, vol 20, no 2, pp 170-174, January 2009.

[18] For an introduction to the subject, go to www.lovemeditating.com/how-to-practice-buddhist-meditation

[19] See, for example, SHARMA, Manoj, and RUSH, Sarah E., "Mindfulness-Based Stress Reduction as a Stress Management Intervention for Healthy Individuals", *Journal of Evidence-Based Complementary and Alternative Medicine*, vol 19, no 4, pp 271-286, October 2014.

[20] See www.careeraddict.com/corporate-philanthropy

[21] See www.wonderslist.com/top-10-most-charitable-people

[22] See www.worldatlas.com/articles/the-10-most-generous-countries

[23] BUBER, Martin, *Ich und Do (I and Thou)*, first published in German in 1923, latest reprint in English by Simon & Schuster, 1996.

[24] KANT, Immanuel, *Groundwork of the Metaphysic of Morals*, 1785, in which he introduces the concept of "categorical imperative".

[25] See, for example, GIDDENS, Prof Anthony, *The Third Way*, 2nd edn, Polity Press, 2011.

[26] MASON, Paul, "The End of Capitalism Has Begun", *The Guardian*, 17th July 2015.

[27] ELLEN MACARTHUR FOUNDATION report, "A New Textiles Economy: Redesigning Fashion's Future", 2017.

[28] ELLEN MACARTHUR FOUNDATION report, "Rethinking the Future of Plastics", 2016.

[29] ELLEN MACARTHUR FOUNDATION report, "Towards the Circular Economy, Vol 2", 2013.

[30] PODSAKOFF, Nathan P., WHITING, Steven W., PODSAKOFF, Philip M., and BLUME, Brian D., "Individual- and Organizational-Level Consequences of Organizational Citizenship Behaviors: A Meta-Analysis", *Journal of Applied Psychology*, vol 94, no 1, January 2009.

[31] See, for example, GARTON, Eric, and MANKINS, Michael, "Engaging Your Employees Is Good, But Don't Stop There", *Harvard Business Review*, 9th December 2015.

[32] "Charitable Giving Boosts SMEs' Bottom Line", www.smallbusiness.co.uk

[33] GREENLEAF, Robert K., *Servant Leadership*, Paulist Press Int, 1977.

[34] GRANT, Adam, *Give and Take*, published by W & N, 2014.

www.ingramcontent.com/pod-product-compliance
Lightning Source LLC
Chambersburg PA
CBHW071625080526
44588CB00010B/1271